STRIKING
SUCCULENT
GARDENS

STRIKING SUCCULENT GARDENS

Plants and Plans for Designing Your Low-Maintenance Landscape

GABRIEL FRANK

PHOTOGRAPHS BY DAN KURAS

TEN SPEED PRESS
California | New York

CONTENTS

PREFACE   vii

INTRODUCTION: **Down the Garden Path** 1

CHAPTER 1: **Small Spaces** 11

CHAPTER 2: **Outdoor Container Gardens** 25

CHAPTER 3: **Saucers, Platters, and Pinwheels** 41

CHAPTER 4: **Aloe, What's Your Name?** 59

CHAPTER 5: **The Spiny Side** 83

CHAPTER 6: **Fusion Gardens** 111

CHAPTER 7: **Tools, Techniques, and Plant Care** 133

CHAPTER 8: **Propagation** 159

COLD-HARDY SUCCULENTS 166

RESOURCES 169

ACKNOWLEDGMENTS 172

ABOUT THE AUTHOR 174

INDEX 175

This book is dedicated to my parents,
Mark and Laure Frank, who seeded in me
an insatiable curiosity for plants and
the natural world from a young age.

PREFACE

To be perfectly honest, succulents were not my first botanical crush, or even my second. My journey down the horticulture path has been a marvelous but meandering one filled with discoveries as well as detours. It took a solid decade of working through infatuations with edible plants, tropical orchids, alpine plants from the high country, and delicate ferns from the understory to meet, explore, and ultimately cement my relationship with succulents.

Studying arid-climate plants in the Enid A. Haupt Conservatory at the New York Botanical Garden didn't prepare me for the scale and stature of these plants in their native habitats. It took my moving to the golden hills of Coastal California to witness succulent plants in their element and embrace their bold aesthetic as part of my design repertoire.

As a landscape contractor transplanted to the West Coast from the wet, humid summers of the East, I observed the respective needs of homeowners coast to coast and their landscapes, which were poignantly different and strikingly apparent. Drought-prone areas in the western states require conservative rationing of water and a conscious commitment to use only what is needed. This is where succulents, plants that store copious amounts of water within their tissues, really shine.

New to California and curious about the hydration limits of succulent plants, I planted a few experiments in my own garden. One year, after a good winter rain, I vowed not to water them throughout the coming dry months, to see how these plants would fare until winter rains returned. As the dry summer wore on, I held back the hose to see what materialized. Perennials withered, most grasses flopped flat, and even supposedly hardy shrubs went south. Meanwhile, aloes and agaves, cotyledon and crassula scrunched their leaves up tight, bracing for these lean times. Six months later, when the seasonal rains returned, the majority of survivors were the succulents. Many so-called drought-tolerant plants didn't rebound from my induced dry spell, but the succulents that appeared on death's doorstep plumped up like muffins in

Encephalartos horridus on left and *Aloe excelsa* 'Orange' on right use little water and pair nicely with their similar forms and contrasting texture.

the oven, looking barely worse for wear. It was hard to overlook how the resurrective qualities these plants possessed closely aligned with the extended wet and dry cycles of drought-prone regions.

Little by little, my palette of usable plants expanded to encompass genera from the five Mediterranean-climate regions around the globe: Coastal California, Central Chile, the South African Cape, the Mediterranean Basin, and southwestern Australia. It became my labor of love, but also a necessity, to grade them for their unique qualities, sharp looks, and durability in the garden. My goal was to design with a quiver of striking and suitable succulents that wouldn't slow down a garden's beauty, potential, and power—even in the unpampered gardens of the average time-limited homeowner.

Gardening in the West has taught me many things about water conservation, seasonal rain patterns, microclimates, and the adaptive nature of water-wise plants. I've learned that each succulent is a living reservoir that optimally meters its resources in sync with the environment. When rains are plentiful, growth is lush, blooms fire off, and the plant party ensues. As soil dries out, water and energy are stowed away for the long haul. In a way, the simplicity of succulent plants takes much of the gardener's work out of the equation. These plants are survivors that have eked out genius methods of self-preservation in strenuous climates.

Succulents are not only visually captivating, but they provide solutions for how to interface with the changing conditions of our planet on a daily basis. They provide a simple mantra for keeping in tune with one another and with our environment at large: use resources wisely, celebrate when abundance is present, and keep packing the root cellar for the future. The book you hold is an exploration of this ethos, gleaned from these wondrous plants.

ABOVE: Low-growing coral aloes (*Aloe striata*) surround a sunset patio.

OPPOSITE: Parry's agave (*Agave parryi*), *Aeonium* 'Sunburst', and *Leucadendron* 'Pom Pom' border one end of a bocce court.

Down the Garden Path

Regardless of the color of your thumb, you'll find that succulent plants are an intriguing bunch. Appealing to both the design world and dirt gardeners alike, succulents are one of the few types of plants that offer a variety of striking forms and vivid colors, along with a vibrant presence. Even folks who aren't initially captivated by their visual spell are curious about their ease of care and sparse needs for water and tending. With built-in water storage, succulents are able to thrive in a surprisingly diverse range of climates around the globe, from dense jungles, to scorching deserts, to a host of unforgiving environments in between.

Although succulent plants are not a silver bullet for every application, one of their best features is being adaptable to challenging conditions in which other plants struggle. Shallow soil depths in containers or nutrient-lean soils don't pose problems, as these conditions are similar to the difficulties succulents regularly face in their native rocky environments. And once plants are established, they don't need regular watering, because succulents carefully self-regulate with onboard water reservoirs during dry times. This means, for example, that you can leave for vacation and not worry about returning to a dehydrated garden! Compared to a traditional garden, you don't need to expend much time and energy to keep them looking attractive throughout the year. Succulents are welcome as a user-friendly addition to any garden to provide a functional fit for our time- and resource-starved landscapes.

In this book, I'll introduce you to some of the best types of succulents for your landscape, including the friendly rosette forms, striking aloes, sculptural agaves, and misunderstood cacti. I'll provide examples and advice for incorporating them into your garden (including small spaces), mixing them with non-succulents, and growing them in containers. I've included information on succulent care to help you keep your plants healthy and happy, and on propagation so that you can grow new plants for yourself and your friends. In addition, step-by-step projects are included throughout the book, as well as tips on basic design principles—from scale and contrast, to texture and rhythm—so that you can understand how to think like a garden designer and plan the succulent garden of your dreams.

But before we begin, let's make a pit stop to clarify the three overarching concepts that are often misunderstood. Although succulents are simple in nature, they're easily confused with regard to their garden applications. It's time to set the record straight.

Are Succulents and Cacti the Same?

OPPOSITE: Classic columnar cacti-form of monstrose apple cactus (*Cereus peruvianus* f. *monstrose*) Below: *Echeveria* 'Ruffles' in front, *Agave desmetiana* 'Variegata' in back

Although these two types of plants are commonly lumped together, they have important differences that set them apart. The helpful riddle that both separates and relates the two is this: all cacti are succulents, but not all succulents are cacti. The word "succulent" stems from the Latin *succus*, meaning juice or sap, and all plants that store an abundance of liquid in their flesh can be considered succulents—including cacti. Cacti fall into the succulent category at large because of their ability to store water, but they have developed specific physical features, namely areoles—the buds from which primarily spines grow (see photo, page 94)—that distinguish them as a unique family of plants: Cactaceae.

You can think of cacti as the most intrepid division of the succulent tribe, sent to conquer the driest climates on Earth. Taming this austere world took some significant anatomical upgrades over several millennia. True leaves were shed and thickened, and armored stems became the primary surface for photosynthesis. Areoles developed on the stems as distinct buds from which spines, flowers, or branches arise. No other family of plants besides cacti possess areoles, so their presence is a standout feature from other succulent families. The layout of areoles across the stem often forms striking geometric patterns, enabling an impressive defense system of clustered spines. Barrel cacti (*Echinocactus* spp.), hedgehog cacti (*Echinopsis* spp.), and prickly pear cacti (*Opuntia* spp.) have particularly prominent areoles. To learn more about areoles and the cacti clan, see chapter 5, The Spiny Side.

Garden Design Tips: Rhythm

For all the wildness, freedom, and organic character that the garden embodies, landscapes benefit from repeating elements that contribute unity to the space. An understandable folly of the beginning gardener is to fall in love with every species and include them all, so the landscape becomes a curio cabinet of plants lacking direction and theme. Carrying a theme through the garden by means of repetition creates an essential sense of movement and unity. Texture, form, contrast, and color are all repeatable themes that have a strong influence in leading the viewer through the space. When the eye recognizes the repetition of particular plants or design themes, a sense of rhythm is achieved.

The garden pictured here features plants displaying variations on a theme. Succulents with thin linear leaves form the bones of the arrangement, starting with a pair of trunky yuccas flanking the entry to the red cottage. Each globe-shaped head is composed of hundreds of narrow leaves, their fine texture highlighted against the barn-red paint. A ground-hugging *Agave geminiflora* echoes the yucca's texture.

A large clump of *Agave* 'Blue Flame' provides contrasting density with its colonizing habit, and weights the center of the plantings. Behind the agave, variegated ribbons of foliage from *Beaucarnea* 'Gold Star' vibe off its taller and wider-leafed cousin to the right—*Beaucarnea guatemalensis*. The similar spray of foliage atop a trunk unites the group of *Beaucarnea* with the yucca, rounding out the look. Lower to the earth, groupings of *Echeveria* 'Lipstick' pop though the silver carpet of *Dymondia margaretae* that softens the flagstones' edges. Flow is created throughout the space as the silver carpet wraps both edges of the flagstone, making the path feel wider.

Succulents Don't Need or Like Water, Right?

Behind succulents' rise to fame is their ease of culture and low water needs. Succulents *do*, indeed, need and enjoy occasional water, but the amount and timing of application are important considerations, so the gardener must strike a balance between conservation and dehydration.

Succulents' root systems tend to be more wide than deep, spreading laterally to soak up shallow, infrequent rains. Internal cells within the plants' flesh plump up fully with water after a soak, and these onboard reserves keep the plants alive until another shower refills the tank. In areas where succulents grow naturally, dry periods can extend for weeks, months, or seasons, depending on the climate. Because of these arid origins, succulent roots appreciate dry periods between waterings, which is why specialized potting mixes are grainy, coarse, and well-draining. Like good house guests respect their welcome windows, succulent roots prefer water to visit briefly, soak in, and continue on. Extended periods of water without relief lead to root rot and deterioration. Detailed instructions on the art of watering are provided on pages 142–146.

Can I Grow Succulents if I Don't Live in a Desert?

Absolutely! Succulents have been pegged as desert dwellers, but they actually have a broad growing range throughout every continent except Antarctica. Although a majority of succulents inhabit dry regions, many species are from tropical, temperate, and mountain communities. The thread-leaved mistletoe cactus (*Rhipsalis cereuscula*), for example, is a common resident of steamy tree canopies in tropical forests of the Caribbean and the Americas, while the San Pedro cactus (*Echinopsis pachanoi*) and the old man of the mountain cactus (*Oreocerus* spp.) inhabit territories in the Andes from 3,000 to 10,000 feet.

In recent years, intrepid North American gardeners have pushed the envelope by growing succulents in wetter and colder climates, such as those in the Pacific Northwest, the Mid-Atlantic region, the Gulf Coast, Canada, and the Carolinas. A few succulents are indigenous to these areas, but gardeners are demonstrating that many more are surprisingly hardy outside their expected range. Would you guess that a multitude of sedums are native to Washington, Oregon, alpine regions in the Cascade Range, and even British Columbia? Broadleaf stonecrop (*Sedum spathulifolium*), Pacific stonecrop (*S. divergens*), wormleaf stonecrop (*S. stenopetalum*), and Oregon stonecrop (*S. oreganum*), in addition to many species of hens and chicks (genus *Sempervivum*) and hardy ice plants (genus *Delosperma*), will cheerily blaze through whiteout storms provided they have decent drainage. On the opposite side of the country, gardeners in the Mid-Atlantic and Northeast have been gradually lifting the succulent ban, bringing handfuls of agave, yucca, and cacti through snowy USDA Zone 5 to 7 winters. (The US Department of Agriculture, or USDA, publishes a zone map of the United States that serves as the standard for determining which plants will thrive in which locations. USDA zones are based on average winter temperatures.)

Juniper Level Botanic Garden in North Carolina is a both a pioneer demonstration garden and a fabulous nursery (Plant Delights) that has been trialing unique and unusual succulents and plants of all origins since 1988. Many exciting cold-hardy agave and yucca selections have been developed and made available through the nursery's mail-order channel and open-garden programs.

Aloe species and other succulents thrive on the coastal bluff.

Farther northwest, in the bone-chilling mountains of the Dakotas and Montana, native cacti genera *Echinocereus*, *Pediocactus*, *Escobaria*, and *Opuntia* provide unthinkably hardy candidates for weather in the most frigid Zone 4 climates (from -25° to -30°F). Because of a shorter growing season, these cacti are naturally smaller species, but they nevertheless provide great opportunities to add cacti to gardens in almost any climate.

In great thanks to the bold efforts of Greg Starr (Starr Nursery), Tony Avent (Plant Delights Nursery), Kelly Griffin (Altman Plants), Brian Kemble (Ruth Bancroft Garden), John Trager (The Huntington Botanical Gardens), Robert Nold, the late Claude Barr (South Dakota plantsman), and other unsung heroes of plant growing and breeding, a swelling repository of distinctive species continue to enlarge the planting possibilities of gardeners in challenging climates. For a detailed list of cold-hardy succulents, see pages 166–67, and for advice on succulent container gardens in cold climates, see page 27.

· · ·

No matter where you live and garden, I hope this book will provide information to help you embrace the beauty of succulents. I have yet to find a more enchanting category of plants that ask for so little to thrive. May you enjoy the journey of welcoming these extraordinary plants into your garden and life.

RIGHT: *Aeonium* 'Sunburst'

OPPOSITE: *Aloe elegans*

CHAPTER 1

Small Spaces

When I lived in Manhattan, and I mentioned that I was a gardener, I received the most peculiar responses. Despite there being many public parks in New York City, some people weren't sure that plants would thrive in the city and wondered how my profession was even possible there. "Gahdening in New Yawk City?" they would echo with a baffled look. Their assertions were good backup that I was on the right track, as I inherently knew the city needed the balance of visible green spaces more desperately than many other areas. Indeed, many plants grow in New York City gardens and parks, but they are freely overlooked within the urban matrix. Tucked away on private rooftop gardens, courtyards, and windy fire escapes, many prized leafy holdouts are doing quite well.

While attending the School of Professional Horticulture at New York Botanical Garden, I started Gardens by Gabriel as a one-man landscape design and build outfit. Gardening among the snug townhouse quarters of Greenwich Village, my love of plants translated into the art of designing with them. Townhouses were tall and narrow, squashed-together buildings with the blessing of a ground floor garden and a roof deck, if you were lucky. Any open patch of earth was highly prized as a personal retreat from the city's everyday bustle. In such a compact space, every inch counts, so my designs were careful exercises in maximizing the potential of pocket-sized real estate. Each shrub, vine, pebble, and piece of pottery had to contribute a strong purpose in bringing life to the space in the best proportions. There was no room for filler, and plants not pulling their weight were composted without reservation. These personal spaces were curated, just as neighboring art galleries were. The experience of working in these niche habitats, which often served as the sole connection people had to the natural world, was invaluable to me and brought a great appreciation of gardening small for big impact.

Bold rosettes of dinner plate aeonium (*Aeonium urbicum*) and penwiper plant (*Kalanchoe marmorata*) hold the foreground and weave together with the wavy fronds of foxtail ferns (*Asparagus densiflorus* 'Myers'), sedums, and blooming lavender scallops (*Kalanchoe fedtschenkoi*) in this small and restful retreat.

With urban and denser suburbs becoming the norm, small to modest-sized residential lots are a reality for many. Large gardens can be impressive to visit and great for taking in sweeping views, but humans gravitate toward spaces that feel intimate and protected. You could think of any planned landscape, no matter how grandiose, as being an aggregate of smaller garden rooms and features, with transitions between them. The good news is that design principles stay constant, so many landscape tactics can be applied to postage stamp–sized plots with similar effect. Creating points of interest, vignettes, and moments within the garden is the real challenge in making a smaller space feel dynamic.

Following are a few techniques for making the most of compact quarters.

Draw it out. Space is always critical, especially when it's tight, so do yourself the favor of making a simple sketch to ensure that all the functional ingredients and plants you have in mind will fit. Use a ruler to get the appropriate scale of 1 inch = 4 feet (called $^1/_4$-inch scale), or download one of the free programs available for simple computer drafting. (SketchUp Free, for example, is a good three-dimensional modeling application if you have digital inclinations for rendering space.) If DIY is your chosen route, draw out the space to scale and play with the proportions of design elements. This enables you to create a mockup of everyday usable features (such as patio, table, grill, and fire pit) before you bring plants into the equation. Once you've nailed down the spots for furniture and features, you'll find it easier to beautify and enhance the space with surrounding plants. For a more crafty hands-on approach, cut out scaled shapes from colored paper to represent garden features and move them around your base drawing to see how everything mingles.

Welcome to the jungle. Building a botanical tapestry within a petite garden can create big impact by interweaving texture, shape, and color. Succulents are perfect for layering together in tight quarters and don't mind any bits of shade they cast upon one another, as long as they receive a solid half-day of sun. Try shoehorning together taller aeoniums, kalanchoes, and blue chalk fingers (*Senecio vitalis*) with colorful echeverias, graptopetalums, jade plants (*Crassula* spp.), and portulacarias to create a seven-layer cake. When plants get too leggy, you can easily cut them back to create fresh propagation stock that you can plug right in or plant in other areas (for more on propagation, see chapter 8). Don't be afraid to double-down with other highly textured water-wise plants such as ornamental grasses, shrubs, and perennials for a fusion effect. Species with oversized leaves, such as Japanese aralia (*Fatsia* spp.), cabbage palm (*Cordyline* spp.), and astelia can be added to provide great contrast

to beadlike succulent foliage. On the flipside, fine-foliaged companions such as the dwarf clumping bamboo *Chusquea coronalis*, little river wattles (*Acacia cognata* 'Cousin Itt'), wax flowers (*Chamelaucium* spp.), and dainty *Lophomyrtus* species provide a soft foil for chunky echeverias, aloes, and agaves planted in the foreground.

Use pottery and bold accents. In addition to adding vertical interest and splashes of color, pots provide growing spaces for plants beyond the soil. In fact, a lush garden can be fashioned strictly using containers if no open ground is available. Lightweight resin containers are readily available in a variety of traditional and trough styles and can add instant growing spaces and aesthetic upgrades. As design features, brightly glazed pots or distinctive art objects can significantly up the ante on a planting combination, creating flexible focal points that can be moved if desired. Think of additional elements such as fencing, outdoor rugs, and accent walls as forming the frame and layered backdrop for your garden's plant portrait. An accent wall painted a dark or neutral color can provide a clean canvas for vibrant foliage. Likewise, using slats of horizontal wood or corrugated metal as a background brings every plant forward into focus.

Garden Design Tips: Form, Texture, and Contrast

Imagine a landscape in black and white—think only about the relative shapes and textures of the plants and objects in grayscale. Those shapes and textures are just as essential, if not more, than the landscape's true colors found in real life. Color is ephemeral, coming and going through the seasons, but a garden that radiates form and texture has depth throughout the year. Visual texture is the perceived quality of a surface, as opposed to how the surface actually feels. Texture links with emotion and is one of the first things we notice. Fine, fuzzy textures in succulents like the panda plant (*Kalanchoe tomentosa*) or the chenille plant (*Echeveria pulvinata*) emit a warm, inviting response and beg to be touched. The coarse and edgy consistency of chunky agave foliage gives us pause before approaching.

The visual surface, shape, size, and weight of plants contribute qualities that range from coarse to fine, and light to heavy. Large and boldly shaped leaves are considered "coarse" in the world of horticulture while slender wispy leaves are considered "fine." Aeoniums and most aloes would therefore be coarse, while portulacaria and groundcover sedums with tiny leaves are fine.

Contrast is created when coarse or heavy textured surfaces are juxtaposed against light ones. Underplanting bold rosettes with finer *Sempervivum*, *Delosperma*, *Sedum* 'Angelina', or a fine gravel gives an enticing touch to a composition. Perennials, grasses, and reeds with wispy stems carry a finer texture, so these are invaluable as textural counterpoints to heavy or coarse plants, bringing drama to the mixed garden.

The small garden pictured opposite is a study in texture and contrast. Whale's tongue agave (*Agave ovatifolia*) sports one of the broadest leaves of the genus, providing a bold anchor for the vignette. Oversized, toothy foliage gives it a solid presence. Arching from behind like a crashing wave is a clump of Mexican weeping bamboo (*Otatea acuminata aztecorum*) with its feathery, layered foliage. Its slender leaves and thin canes shift in the slightest breeze, creating a kinetic backdrop. Its texture is light but also rich, with many layers of foliage that create depth. The matte blue wall of the house behind heightens the contrast of coarse and fine values of these two specimens. A midground fence panel contributes lateral movement along the ground plane, offering a break from the skyward reaching agave and yucca in the foreground. *Yucca* Bright Star catches the eye with its luminescent yellow variegation and sword-shaped leaves. Its texture is more airy than the agave but denser than the bamboo, providing necessary balance.

A smooth stucco backdrop enhances the bristly texture of the upright cardon cactus (*Pachycereus pringlei*) and bromeliads in this narrow planting space.

Create a nook. A garden room can be any space that provides a sense of privacy or feels separate from the rest of the garden. A hammock between two trees, a chair hidden behind a wispy bamboo, and a sunken garden are all places to steal away and crack a book or just sit in silence. Make the most of a golden opportunity by using solid or semipermeable panels, vertical screening plants, oversized planters, or changes in elevation to set off a part of the garden for a garden room. Partially obscuring a view creates a sense of drama, as what lies beyond is a mystery. One of the best tips for making a space feel larger is to include at least one garden room.

• • •

You may find that creating a garden in a small space is actually more fun and less intimidating than working in a large plot. Having less real estate to cover means you can focus on fewer elements and helps you decisively dial-in the garden's look and feel. Tackling even the smallest spaces builds your confidence for jumping to the next swath ahead, so piecemeal can be a good way to go for a DIY garden.

The projects ahead are meant to illustrate how crafting a small garden can be rewarding, and that great things do come in petite packages.

Secret Passage

A MINIATURE PINE TREE
(*Crassula tetragona*)

B MOTHER OF THOUSANDS
(*Kalanchoe daigremontiana*)

C BLACK ROSE AEONIUM
(*Aeonium 'Zwartkop'*)

D BLUE CHALK STICKS
(*Senecio mandraliscae*)

E GIANT VELVET ROSE
(*Aeonium canariense*)

F GHOST PLANT
(*Graptopetalum
paraguayense*)

Many front approaches to homes sadly leave little room for a planted environment to guide your passage. Fortunately for succulent fans, we have lots of successful plant options when it comes to the challenge of container planting and cramped front walkway beds.

This project creates a garden flanking a narrow entryway to a house, in beds less than a foot wide, yet an abundance of succulents has been used to create a lush composition. In any narrow space, the key to making the planting area feel dynamic is to mix up the plant heights and textures.

Amend the soil with 2 to 6 inches of well-finished compost (see pages 134–37).

Miniature pine trees and mother of thousands are slender, upright growers that provide the texture of a sculpted bonsai. In this narrow planting, place them against the wall midway down the path, behind lower growing plants so their height doesn't block small succulents and so they stand out as focal points.

Plant a richly colored black rose aeonium next to the miniature pine and mother of thousands, as these will also grow taller over time. The dark burgundy aeonium foliage provides contrast to the blues and greens of the other plants, making the color appear even more saturated.

Moving outward from the taller succulents, intersperse blue chalk stick plants with pinwheel-shaped velvet roses. Blue chalk sticks contribute their sapphire color and open, twiggy texture to the composition, while the repetition of mint-green velvet roses in this small space gives weight to the presentation.

Tuck in smoky, pink ghost plants along the outer edges of the planting and among the larger succulents to accent the larger rosettes and provide further contrast to the blue and green hues.

Succulent Tapestry

A TOOTHLESS TORCH ALOE
(*Aloe arborescens* 'Spineless')

B QUIVER TREE
(*Aloe dichotoma*)

C CHIMANIMANI ALOE
(*Aloe munchii*)

D FRENCH ALOE
(*Aloe pluridens*)

E HUMMEL'S SUNSET JADE PLANT
(*Crassula ovata* 'Hummel's Sunset')

F GHOST PLANT
(*Graptopetalum paraguayense*)

G JELLY BEAN STONECROP
(*Sedum pachyphyllum*)

H COPPERTONE STONECROP
(*Sedum nussbaumerianum*)

I PORK AND BEANS STONECROP
(*Sedum rubrotinctrum*)

J BLUE SPRUCE STONECROP
(*Sedum reflexum* 'Blue Spruce')

A small space can carry a mighty impact, as evidenced by Stacy Peralta's wall-to-wall succulent scramble in Cayucos, California. An avid aloe collector, he's managed to pack in a diverse collection of choice aloe species and groundcover succulents that carpet a modest 20-by-30-foot front yard. Tree aloe varieties (some of Stacy's own hybrids) provide good scale and dominate the skyline, while shrubby succulent types add structure to the perimeter. Though the aloes are impressive, you can use a rainbow of plants in the Crassulaceae (aka Crassula, or stonecrop) plant family to knit together a tapestry of color and draw the viewer into the intricate space. Along with the strong diversity of creeping succulents, repeated groupings of particular plants throughout the garden provide continuity. The pathway draws the eye through the scene, and the dense pools of sedums and graptopetalums in and around the path create an impression that the stepping stones are floating in a sea of succulents. This garden is an excellent example of how to showcase a polymorphous collection of succulents in an everyday front yard garden.

Amend the soil with 2 to 6 inches of well-finished compost (see pages 134–37).

Spread a 3-inch layer of decomposed granite to create a pathway to a reading bench. (See photo page 23.) Lay pieces of quartzite flagstone over the decomposed granite. This path will provide access to the plants for occasional maintenance.

Plant taller tree aloes and shrubby succulents such as Chimanimani aloe, quiver trees, toothless torch aloe, French aloe, and Hummel's Sunset jade plant on the perimeter. If your garden is fairly open to the street or to neighboring yards, they provide some visual relief and privacy.

Midway down the path, place a Hummel's Sunset jade plant to provide interest and break up the flat carpeting of groundcover plants (see photo, opposite).

To create the stonecrop carpet along the pathway, plant pinkish ghost plants, pale green jelly bean stonecrop, glowing coppertone stonecrop, and pork and beans stonecrop along the sides of the path. Between the flagstone pavers, plant low-slung pork and beans stonecrop and chalk-colored Blue Spruce stonecrop. Use 2- to 3-inch plugs of all these plants, spaced at 12- to 18-inch intervals. It may seem far apart at first, but these spreading groundcovers grow quickly, and their older leaves will fall to the ground and root in time, filling any gaps.

Around the bench, dig in more clumps of jelly bean stonecrop and jewel-toned ghost plants for continuity.

CHAPTER 2

Outdoor Container Gardens

The marvel of cultivating plants in containers harks back to the fabled Hanging Gardens of Babylon, one of the ancient Seven Wonders of the World. Built by King Nebuchadnezzar II during his reign from 605 to 562 BCE, this major engineering feat involved the erection of a majestic tapestry of containerized plants surrounding a stately palace, possibly along the River Euphrates. The story goes that the king had the gardens created to help his wife overcome her homesickness for the lush landscapes in her home country of northern Iran.

Although container materials and methods have morphed over the centuries, the beauty of contained cultivation has remained constant. Containers provide invaluable solutions for growing plants beyond the constraints of location, climate, and season. The vessel, its contents, and the surrounding microclimate become a highly portable gardening experiment. Any environmental issues with water, sun, or airflow can be modified quickly with a change in setting, plant species, or soil type. Containers expand the possibilities of keeping plant allies with you, wherever life leads. If astronauts can grow lettuce and mizuna (Japanese greens) in containers on the International

OPPOSITE: A menagerie of sedums and variegated elephant food (*Portulacaria* 'Variegata') overflow a recycled planter.

RIGHT: Blue chalks sticks (*Senecio mandraliscae*), Echeveria 'Perle von Nurnberg', ghost plant (*Graptopetalum paraguayense*), and pork and beans stonecrop (*Sedum rubrotinctum*) knit together happily.

Space Station, it's no stretch to realize that anyone on Earth can succeed with container culture.

Succulents are able solutions to the challenges of growing plants in the dry soil and confined space of containers. Being natural survivors, succulents will quickly colonize a "closed system," despite any deficiencies in soil nutrients and water, while many other plants would languish and lose vitality in the same environment.

Survival-savvy succulents require less water and nutrients, and they are able to tap into their internal stores slowly as conditions become trying, parceling out resources as needed. Your grandma's heirloom jade plant, *Aloe vera*, or fuzzy old man cactus, *Cephalocereus*, can last for decades in a modest-sized container by carefully consuming reserves stored in its tissues. Although every plant that survives to travel with you (or your grandma) through life eventually needs to be repotted, succulents have the resiliency required to endure the extended spaces in between.

Short-term "contained gardens," such as table centerpieces, holiday wreaths, and wedding boutonnieres, can be composed of all succulents for a fresh approach, shaking up the decorative scene. Beyond the eye candy provided by such arrangements, the sustainability of succulents used in crafts is most surprising. Once the succulents outgrow a small container, or at the close of the event, you can transplant the cuttings directly in the ground or into a larger container to give them a new lease on life. I have created many simple arrangements as demonstrations or as gifts, which have formed blooming colonies after they were transplanted into the landscape.

Beyond their functional aspects, sleek, colorful, rustic, or vintage containers can create an eye-catching aesthetic in the garden. Standing proud, holding a choice plant on a pedestal, a container can serve as an art form along with its contents. The popularity of container

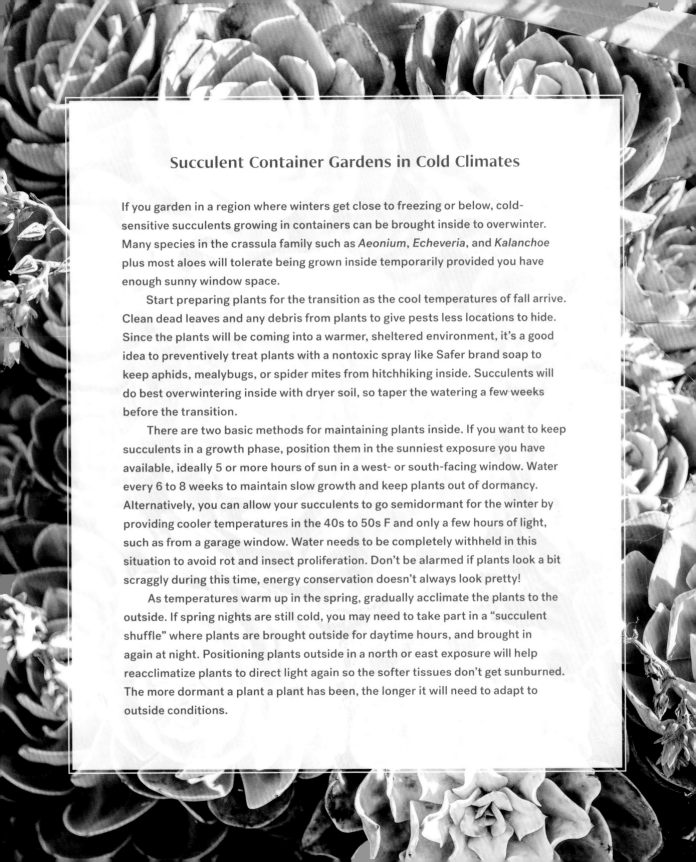

Succulent Container Gardens in Cold Climates

If you garden in a region where winters get close to freezing or below, cold-sensitive succulents growing in containers can be brought inside to overwinter. Many species in the crassula family such as *Aeonium*, *Echeveria*, and *Kalanchoe* plus most aloes will tolerate being grown inside temporarily provided you have enough sunny window space.

Start preparing plants for the transition as the cool temperatures of fall arrive. Clean dead leaves and any debris from plants to give pests less locations to hide. Since the plants will be coming into a warmer, sheltered environment, it's a good idea to preventively treat plants with a nontoxic spray like Safer brand soap to keep aphids, mealybugs, or spider mites from hitchhiking inside. Succulents will do best overwintering inside with dryer soil, so taper the watering a few weeks before the transition.

There are two basic methods for maintaining plants inside. If you want to keep succulents in a growth phase, position them in the sunniest exposure you have available, ideally 5 or more hours of sun in a west- or south-facing window. Water every 6 to 8 weeks to maintain slow growth and keep plants out of dormancy. Alternatively, you can allow your succulents to go semidormant for the winter by providing cooler temperatures in the 40s to 50s F and only a few hours of light, such as from a garage window. Water needs to be completely withheld in this situation to avoid rot and insect proliferation. Don't be alarmed if plants look a bit scraggly during this time, energy conservation doesn't always look pretty!

As temperatures warm up in the spring, gradually acclimate the plants to the outside. If spring nights are still cold, you may need to take part in a "succulent shuffle" where plants are brought outside for daytime hours, and brought in again at night. Positioning plants outside in a north or east exposure will help reacclimatize plants to direct light again so the softer tissues don't get sunburned. The more dormant a plant a plant has been, the longer it will need to adapt to outside conditions.

gardening has brought a host of clever material options to the market that are both lightweight and crack-resistant, compared to yesterday's terra cotta and heavy concrete containers. Where high-fired ceramics have been the standard, companies such as Veradek and PurePots now provide containers composed of sleek, low-density polyethylene (LDPE) resin, metal, and fiberglass. These lightweight materials stand up well to outdoor conditions and are available in attractive finishes.

Lightweight composite and metal containers are very functional for large-scale applications, rooftop gardens, or even back patios. Containers with 3- to 6-foot root space capacities are large enough to accommodate tree aloes and larger species for years, without needing transplanting. Catering to residential use, creative collections of cubes, L-shape planters, spheres, and narrow troughs provide attractive pots for almost any location.

Container gardening is a low-commitment exercise and a good way to start mixing things up with succulents. Try your hand with a few foolproof varieties of succulents, such as those included in the following lists, and let them knit together naturally. Experiment with color themes: assemble one container with warm foliage tones, and create another cool container with blues and purples. It's hard to go wrong with succulents, whose bold looks are easy to arrange harmoniously in a container.

Follow these guidelines to create an attractive, classic thrillers/chillers/spillers–style container combination:

THRILLERS: Place tall plants or objects in the center of the composition to capture attention. Many *Kalanchoe* and *Euphorbia* forms provide strong verticality. Try these selections as centerpieces.

- **Stalactite plant** (*Kalanchoe beharensis* 'Fang') This felted sensation has cupped, bicolor leaves that beg to be touched. Upper leaf surfaces are bronzy, while undersides are downy silver. Fuzzy, pointed bumps resembling fangs or stalactites protrude from the leaf surface, creating a prehistoric presence. (Pictured on page 30, top row, left.)

- **Copper spoons** (*Kalanchoe orgyalis*) If fangs and fuzz aren't your fancy, this species is more refined. A well-branched upright posture and copper-toned leaves give this kalanchoe a classy disposition. (Pictured on page 30, top row, center.)

- **Fire sticks** (*Euphorbia tirucalli* 'Sticks on Fire') An especially fiery form of the standard pencil tree, this plant lights up an arrangement with its coral-like arms that morph between tones of hot pink, red, and yellow. Its vibrant color and upright posture make an ideal centerpiece. (Pictured on page 30, top row, right.)

Build Your Own Metal Planter

If you're drawn to the industrial or vintage look of metal, you can easily fashion your own containers using some basic tools. Cut corrugated or sheet metal to a desired size with a circular saw, tin snips, or an angle grinder fitted with a metal-cutting disc. Build a box frame using rot-resistant wood, and cover it with the metal. Curved and round containers are the easiest to build with metal: simply bend the metal sheet to the desired diameter, overlap the ends, and secure the overlapping portion with self-tapping screws. Corrugations in the metal give the planter rigidity so that no wood frame is needed.

CHILLERS: These friendly plants provide volume and interest to the combination without stealing the show.

- **Afterglow echeveria** (*Echeveria* 'Afterglow') Leaves of this stunning species feature an indescribable color mix of lavender, pink, and blue. This gem of a hybrid glows in containers, plumping to 1 to 2 feet wide when happy. (Pictured opposite, middle row, left.)

- **Elephant food** (*Portulacaria afra* 'Aurea') A more interesting cousin of the common jade, this plant's arching habit contrasts purple stems against golden buttonlike leaves. (Pictured opposite, middle row, center.)

- **Ascot Rainbow spurge** (*Euphorbia* 'Ascot Rainbow') This cold- and heat-hardy selection has a mounded habit with beautifully variegated foliage and flowers. It is equally versatile as a thriller or chiller. (Pictured opposite, middle row, right.)

SPILLERS: Draping plants over a container's rim creates an overflowing feel of abundance and softens up firm edges.

- **Coppertone stonecrop** (*Sedum nussbaumerianum* 'Coppertone') This evergreen sedum features radiant, tangerine-toned leaves. More durable that most sedums, its color really shines in containers. (Pictured opposite, bottom row, left.)

- **Campfire plant** (*Crassula capitella* 'Campfire') A blazing visual fiesta, this plant's whorled leaves freely spiral over the container's edges, blending colors from chartreuse to inferno red. (Pictured opposite, bottom row, center.)

- **Fish hooks** (*Senecio radicans*) Curiously curved, blue-green leaves trail abundantly over any surface. Glaucous foliage gives a cooling contrast to more fiery succulent companions. (Pictured opposite, bottom row, right.)

Although small containers are cute and appealing initially, maintenance needs are far less if you use medium-sized containers with a diameter and depth of 12 to 18 inches. Succulents are tolerant of tiny spaces in the short term, but medium-sized containers offer a decent volume of soil capacity for roots to colonize. A good volume of soil means that plants can flourish for multiple years without needing to be repotted.

In addition, the water-holding capacity of a 12- to 18-inch mass of soil means you'll need to water only once a week if the container is kept in part sun. If you're using smaller containers, if containers are surrounded by heat-reflecting hardscape materials, or if summer days are consistently warmer than 90°F, containers may need watering twice a

week. Adjust your watering schedule to accommodate heat and climate.

With established plants, you should always allow soil to almost dry out, but not fully dry out, before watering containerized succulents. You can check the soil moisture with a moisture meter, or plunge your finger about 3 inches into the soil to gauge the amount of hydration. If it feels dry, add enough water to soak the soil thoroughly. Water lightly with a wand on the diffused shower setting in consecutive round motions to dampen the soil slowly. A mulch of pebbles or other organic materials is always helpful initially to reduce water evaporation from the soil and to keep roots cool until the plants' foliage covers the surface.

Container gardening offers you an opportunity to make a microcosm of the greater landscape in a portable package. Similar to the art of bonsai, you are dwarfing a plant's size by limiting its available root space. Depending on the container size, many succulents will grow out of the arrangement in a few years and will need to be repotted. Until that time, use the close quarters of the pot to display a tapestry of texture and color. Containers are especially welcome to call attention to entryways, as focal points, and in any area that needs a bit of inspiration to stand out. The projects that follow will inspire your own one-of-kind container creations.

Bodhi Bowl

A MIRROR BUSH
(*Coprosma repens* 'Painter's Palette')

B WOOLLY BUSH
(*Adenanthos sericeus*)

C MEXICAN SNOWBALL
(*Echeveria elegans*)

D KIWI AEONIUM
(*Aeonium* 'Kiwi')

E COPPERTONE STONECROP
(*Sedum nussbaumerianum* 'Coppertone')

F STRING OF PEARLS
(*Senecio rowleyanus*)

G GOLDMOSS STONECROP
(*Sedum acre*)

A low, wide dish makes an ideal container for mixing succulent species into a table-worthy arrangement. This enlightened arrangement is centered by a meditative Buddha figure holding a lotus flower, but you can use any small garden sculpture as a centerpiece. Around the Buddha is an array of succulents and dwarf shrubs, suggesting a serene forest scene.

Cover the drainage holes inside the container with mesh drywall tape or screen, and fill the bowl about halfway full with cactus mix or another well-draining soil mix.

Place a Buddha or another statue as a centerpiece.

Use two dwarf shrubs to create structure: add a glossy-leaved mirror bush next to the Buddha and a woolly bush a bit behind the statue as a gauzy backdrop.

Insert clumps of Mexican snowball, Kiwi aeonium, and coppertone stonecrop around the front and sides of the Buddha statue, leaving a couple empty pockets near the front edges of the pot. Add string of pearls and goldmoss stonecrop to the front, draping over the edges of the container.

Once all plants are in place, fill in with potting mix to bring the level about 1 inch from the rim to allow room for the final surface dressing. Use your fingers to pack soil in between plants to push out air gaps.

Use fine gravel, tumbled glass, or other fine-grained material to mulch between the plants, which will eventually grow to cover the entire surface. Beyond looking attractive, the mulch layer helps diffuse water into the pot and protects the soil from escaping the pot.

Discography

A BRITTLE STAR DYCKIA
(*Dyckia* 'Brittle Star')

B STALACTITE PLANT
(*Kalanchoe beharensis* 'Fang')

C DAVID CUMMING GRAPTOVERIA
(× *Graptoveria* 'David Cumming')

D ROSA GRAPTOSEDUM
(× *Graptosedum* 'Rosa')

E DONDO ECHEVERIA
(*Echeveria* 'Dondo')

F MEXICAN SNOWBALL
(*Echeveria elegans*)

G TINY BUTTONS STONECROP
(*Sedum hispanicum*)

H FISH HOOKS
(*Senecio radicans*)

I STRING OF PEARLS
(*Senecio rowleyanus*)

Create this trio of dish planters as an attractive focal point that can be appreciated from inside and out. In the middle of the soil mound, where the soil depth is greatest, you can plant large or striking plants. Arrange a mix of any small- to medium-sized succulents around the central plant to offer color and/or textural themes.

The containers shown here are actually disc blades from a tractor plow, which can be ordered online at an affordable price. These blades are available in various sizes, from 18 to 26 inches, depending on the scale you want for your arrangement. The discs need to be welded onto three, 1- to 2-inch pipes of roughly 18 inches, 24 inches, and 36 inches tall, or you could attach them using heavy-duty construction adhesive or two-part epoxy if welding isn't possible. This assembly does require that you mix and pour concrete (three bags of Quikrete) and use a drill with a bit (such as cobalt) that can drill through metal; enlist help if you're not comfortable doing this yourself.

Start with three pipes of varying heights (as described above). Because about 12 inches of each pipe will be sunk into a concrete footing, at 14 inches from the bottom each pipe, use a marker to indicate placement of two or three, $1/8$-inch drainage holes, which after installation will be about 2 inches above ground level. Then, with a drill bit intended for metal, drill the holes in the pipes.

Dig three holes, each approximately 16 inches deep and wide. Mix one bag of Quikrete according to package instructions and pour the entire mixture into one of the holes. If you're adding an irrigation line (see the following note), fill the hole with 4 inches of concrete and place the conduit and pipe stem in the concrete before pouring in the remainder.

Note: If drip irrigation will be used, you'll need to run $1/4$-inch drip tubing inside $1/2$-inch flexible conduit through the concrete footing and pipe stems, leaving a few feet of tubing exposed at both ends. The conduit will protect the dripline from kinking in the concrete. Work the conduit into the footing when pouring the concrete, leaving a 2-foot tail of irrigation line coming out of the footing to connect to the main $1/2$-inch dripline and about 12 inches of tubing coming out of the top of the pipe, where the disc will be attached. Be careful not to get any concrete inside the irrigation line.

Tape off the drainage holes in the pipes for protection from concrete overspray, and sink one pipe 12 inches into the wet concrete, making sure that the top of the pipe is level and the taped drainage hole stays 2 inches above the surface of the concrete. Fill the remaining holes with concrete and pipes in the same way.

Lay the disc concave-side down on the ground for stability, and drill three, $1/4$-inch holes for drainage spaced about 1 inch apart using a drill bit intended for metal.

The next day, when the concrete has cured around the pipe stems, attach the discs to the top of the pipes by welding, epoxying, or using another fastening technique.

Place a small piece of landscape fabric over the holes in the bottom of each disc to keep soil in place while allowing water to drain. Fill the discs with cactus mix or another well-draining soil mix. Because the discs are shallow, mound up the soil about 2 to 4 inches in the center to provide the maximum amount of soil for root growth.

Place a thriller in the center of each disc: in the tallest disc, a burgundy Brittle Star dyckia resembles a spiny starfish; in the medium-tall disc, a velvet stalactite plant stands proudly; in the lowest disc, a multicolor David Cumming graptoveria fans out.

Next, the chillers. Plant Rosa graptosedum in the tall disc, a ghostly Mexican snowball and green Dondo echeveria in the medium-tall disc, and Dondo echeveria and tiny buttons stonecrop in the lowest disc.

Now for the spillers. Plant fish hooks and string of pearls to spill over the edges of the two tallest discs. Trailing plants are complimentary additions that soften a container's edge.

Once you've finished planting, add soil mix to fill in the gaps between plants, and use your fingers to apply firm pressure to the soil to press out air gaps.

If you're using drip irrigation, add four, $1/2$-gallon-per-hour emitters to the $1/4$-inch drip tubing in the discs and stake the tubing down with landscape staples.

Add beach pebbles or gravel as a top dressing.

x *Graptoveria* 'David Cumming'

CHAPTER 3

Saucers, Platters, and Pinwheels

The gateway into succulent cultivation often begins with what I consider the softer side of the family: aeoniums, echeverias, and dudleyas. These plants belong to the Crassulaceae (stonecrop) family, which includes about 1,500 species. Their symmetrical rosettes of foliage remind me of oversized petals and pinwheels. "It looks just like a flower!" people exclaim when they see a basketball-sized aeonium rosette or tender-leaved echeveria for the first time. As a bonus, these plump foliage-flowers don't last just a week in a vase, but radiate for years in the garden.

Saucers, platters, and pinwheels are delightful shapes for decorating the garden, and they are featured in some of the most carefree succulents for cultivation, whose rounded rosettes multiply every year and whose curious flowers are always a surprise. Whether you're a collector or a novice, you'll find hundreds of species and cultivars to keep things interesting within the ranks of the stonecrop family, from silver-dollar–sized miniatures like Echeveria 'Dondo' to heady saucer plants (Aeonium undulatum), with rosettes the size of dinner plates.

Stonecrops also come in a variety of knockout colors, ranging from the rich burgundies and limey greens of aeoniums, through the jewel-toned pastels of echeverias, to the chalky white and silver of dudleyas. At the nursery, be wise to the "kid in the candy store" effect, because there is undeniably a "collect 'em all!" feeling that builds with each new plant discovery.

While stonecrops share many traits, each has a distinct growth habit, appearance, and cultivation needs. This chapter is organized by genus to highlight the unique characteristics of each and to illustrate their best applications within the garden.

Mexican snowball (Echeveria elegans) colonizes the edge of a gravel path with Echeveria colorata 'Mexican Giant' filling in behind.

LEFT: Giant velvet rose aenonium (*Aeonium canariensis*)

RIGHT: *Aeonium* 'Kiwi'

Aeonium

(*Aeonium* spp.)

Because of their ease of cultivation and propensity to multiply like rabbits, aeoniums are likely the most commonly cultivated succulents. Almost all aeoniums originate from the Canary Islands archipelago off the coast of northwestern Africa, with a few outliers from other African coastal zones with mild, Mediterranean-type climates, dry summers, and wet winters.

Aeoniums are fairly adaptable but perform best in cooler coastal conditions without seasonal temperature extremes. Most species will survive light frosts in the high 20s to low 30s F, but they will be severely damaged or killed if temperatures drop much below that. Hot sun will scorch the foliage and dehydrate the plants—these are not desert dwellers. Sited properly with afternoon shade and some water, they can adapt to warmer regions with temperatures in the low 90s F.

Although most succulents are sun lovers, aeoniums are one of the few that thrive in the shade. They will grow happily under a loose tree canopy or on the shady side of the house, where they receive only a few hours of direct sun. To look their best, garden-grown aeoniums appreciate a little more water than other succulents. A small, fine-textured root system is their weakness, which reduces their ability to collect moisture as the soil dries.

Aeoniums and dudleyas (aka live-forevers) are similar in that they have evolved in coastal Mediterranean climates and are late-fall-to-spring growers, putting forth the largest flushes of growth when conditions are mild and rain is plentiful—usually November to March. Leverage these plants as highlights of the cooler months, because a garden can feature plants that shine throughout the year, not just in the summer. Instead of winter being a dull off-season for gardens, in a Mediterranean climate, many succulents bank energy all year to strut their stuff in the winter and spring, when resources are prime.

The flipside of a garden with cool-season growers is their summer rest, or semidormancy, period. Without summer moisture, aeoniums will enter into a natural survival mode, curling their leaves into a tight rosette to minimize transpiration. Think of mama bear conserving calories while hibernating in a cozy, protected cave. This summer dormancy may seem alarming if you're familiar with traditional cycles of most garden plants, whose rest periods occur in the winter.

Plant dormancy in the garden isn't necessarily a low point and can be accommodated in different ways. Given some water and relief from the hot sun, aeoniums will push through the summer, growing slowly, while still maintaining fairly good looks and not going fully dormant. Planting herbaceous companions that peak in summer, such as the Summer Red conebush (*Leucadendron salignum* 'Summer Red'), flowering Mexican heathers (*Cuphea* spp.), and other drought-tolerant perennials, will help provide garden interest throughout the season.

After dormancy ends in the fall, the aeonium resurrection is a spectacle to behold. Tight fists of foliage that once looked like they'd given up the ghost slip out of a growth coma and inflate like balloons. New, shimmering foliage radiates out from the center rosettes, quickly expanding the plants three to six times the size of their former sleepy selves and returning to the garden party like they never missed a beat.

Saucer plant (*Aeonium undulatum*)

Aeoniums are relatively fast growers, but they can take a few a few years to form a blooming colony. Once the larger selections, such as the saucer plant and the tree aeonium, have tucked away enough energy, they produce impressive, cone-shaped panicles of starry flowers in yellow and creamy shades from winter to spring. The saucer plant, shown on page 43, is a giant of the genus at 6 feet tall, topped by canary-yellow blooms. Purple-foliaged cultivars such as giant red aeoniums (A. 'Cyclops' and A. 'Voodoo'), A. 'Velour', and black rose aeonium (A. 'Zwartkop', pictured on page 18) are midsized at 2 to 3 feet tall, with vibrant yellow flowers that are especially showy against a backdrop of dark leaves.

Denser growing forms that feature smaller to midsized rosettes, such as Kiwi aeonium (A. 'Kiwi' pictured on page 42) or green platters (A. 'Pseudotabuliforme'), are less dramatic in bloom, with flowers held tighter to the plant. Only a few rosettes of these well-branched plants create blooms, leaving the majority of the plants intact to continue growth. These cultivars stay under 12 inches tall and make excellent groundcovers.

Live-forever
(*Dudleya* spp.)

You will find these shining crowns happily growing on high cliffs among boulders, gravel scree, and a smattering of horticultural holdouts. Most members of the genus grow within the fog belt of the Pacific Coast, where temperatures are mild but the land remains sunbaked without rainfall for most of the year. Their habitat stretches along a wide range of the West Coast, from the southern part of Baja California up through Northern California and Oregon and across to the coastal islands. A few species have adapted to the more pressing inland mountain habitats of Arizona and Southern California.

With an uncanny ability to root into tiny crevices that even a seasoned rock climber would have trouble holding on to, young dudleya seedlings are opportunists of the first order. Juvenile plants root into channels with scant organic matter and nutrients, without needing the moist, nutrient-rich environment many other young plants require. Pacific fogs are a saving grace, bathing the otherwise parched soil and plant life with water vapor.

One of the succulent's most ornamental traits—the white, powdery coating, which gives the chalk dudleya (*D. pulverulenta*) its common name—is actually a clever characteristic that enables the plant to conserve water.

This glaucous, waxy coating (called farina) reflects ultraviolet rays and reduces sun intensity and water loss from the leaves. Much like a freshly waxed car, water beads up on the surface of the leaves, diverting moisture away from the plant's crown where rot can happen, and out to perimeter roots where moisture is needed. The farina can actually be wiped off with your hand or dissolved with herbicides and pesticides. Therefore, it's important that you take care to protect this delicate coating when you're watering or planting dudleyas; avoid touching the leaves, and grip the root ball under the leaves as you install plants. To mimic natural conditions in your garden and improve the health of your plants, plant dudleyas in vertical or slanted positions to help steer water away from the crowns of the plants to avoid rot.

Live-forevers are class leaders in plants that truly thrive on independence; they are best left to their own devices with minimal input after they're established. Along with other true California natives, they are genetically hardwired to become dormant during the warm, dry summer months. That's the ideal time for an extended siesta, right? Dormancy is not always beautiful, however, and during this rest period, leaves curl up to reduce the area exposed to the sun. Don't be surprised when your plants look like they need a coffee break. The dormancy is part of the plants' natural cycle; rest assured that they will return to their silvery selves as winter rains return. Keep

LEFT, CLOCKWISE: Chalk dudleya (*Dudleya pulverulenta*), Britton's dudleya (*D. brittonii*), (*D. pachyphytum*)

RIGHT: Britton's dudleya (*Dudleya brittonii*)

LEFT: Chalk dudleya
(*D. pulverulenta*) with
California fuchsia
(*Epilobium*)

RIGHT: Chalk dudleya
in full flower

an eye on your dudleyas as dormancy breaks in the winter; it's a wonder to watch the shriveled clumps of leaves swell to life with seasonal moisture.

During their first year in the ground, however, dudleyas will skip dormancy, growing vigorously and needing water throughout the summer to become well-rooted. After their first year, plants positioned in well-drained soil (on a mound or in containers) will tolerate occasional summer water, but it's best to abstain from watering during dormancy to maintain plant health and longevity. This might be a stretch for many gardeners whose first thought when a plant doesn't seem to be thriving is to add water! But succulents are easy to kill with kindness, so this is a good exercise in restraining the natural urge to oversaturate them.

In the landscape, live-forevers harmonize beautifully, like Simon with Garfunkel, with rocks and gravel. When you're planting a garden that features these plants, think about including stone cobbles, gravel, and boulders in the planting scheme to create ideal growing conditions and a natural-looking habitat. Taking advantage of this succulent's innate ability to root into fissures with minimal soil, you can get creative with plantings. Nooks in dry-stack walls or pockets between boulders with only a small stash of soil are great spots to start young plants. As long as you can deliver occasional water to the plants in the first year (only), they'll establish and root fairly easily.

Beyond planting in crevices and rocky outcroppings, you can stage live-forevers in planting schemes among summer-dry plants such as sages, agaves, sticky monkey flowers, and California fuchsias, which provide a welcome contrast in bloom color, leaf texture, and overall scale. Because hummingbirds love to sip their nectar-rich flowers, dudleyas are good additions to any pollinator or wildlife garden.

In mixed borders, dudleyas take center stage winter through spring as they peak into bloom; during the summer, other perennials, grasses, and shrubs provide the highlights. For a cheerful year-round bluff garden, pair live-forevers with coastal compadres such as red buckwheat, California lilac, manzanita, and wild blue rye grass.

Two main types of dudleya plants are often used in garden applications: branched and unbranched types.

Unbranched plants, such as chalk dudleya (*D. pulverulenta;* pictured opposite, left) and Britton's dudleya (*D. brittonii*; pictured on page 45), are the showiest types, with mostly single large rosettes. These showstoppers act as great stand-alone specimens in containers, along with a prominent rock or cobble clusters to create a colony effect. The big, chalky leaves catch the light, like shimmering stars, in a mixed planting.

Branched forms are the quieter members of the clan that steadily anchor the mountain cliffs and sloping banks of the Pacific Coast. They have a beauty all their own, like silvery sea anemones, with densely packed clusters of red-tipped leaves. Considering the relatively small number of species in the genus, the branched types span diverse regions. Almost all of the eight Channel Islands off the California coast, and Cerros Island off the

TOP: Sea lettuce dudleya (*Dudleya caespitosa*)

BOTTOM: Bright green dudleya (*Dudleya virens*)

Baja California coast, are home to endemic dudleya populations that exist nowhere else. Many of these munchkin-sized species, such as Greene's dudleya (*D. greenei*), munchkin dudleya (*D. gnoma*), and Cedros Island dudleya (*D. pachyphytum*), are considered rare or endangered and are protected by law, as their wild habitats, and therefore numbers, have been compromised. If you favor collectible plants and have an interest in conservation, these unusual beauties are definitely worth seeking out. Responsible nurseries and botanical gardens propagate rare varieties by seed and plants are occasionally available, so watch for them. Motivated gardeners and horticulturists have been instrumental in saving these threatened species from extinction. You can be part of the growing solution!

In the garden setting, branched species make dependable groundcovers and good pocket plants, knitting together rockeries and spilling over walls and containers. Sea lettuce (*D. caespitosa*) and the multiple subspecies of bright green dudleya (*D. virens*) form charming 1- to 3-foot colonies of starry rosettes of green and powdery white. These two species can be found just a few feet from the crashing waves in Big Sur, California, fearlessly tackling the wind and salt spray. If other plants have gotten blown away by coastal conditions and you're ready to give up, these survivalists will be up to the challenge.

OPPOSITE: *Echeveria* x 'Imbricata'

BELOW: *Echeveria* 'Ebony'

Hens and chicks

(*Echeveria* spp.)

If there were royalty in the succulent world, echeverias would easily take the crown. They share traits with other members of the Crassula family but are bestowed with particularly noble qualities. Adjectives such as pearlescent, crystalline, and ethereal come to mind in describing their nuanced features.

Even the name of their chief botanical illustrator, Atanasio Echeverría y Godoy, for whom the plants are named, commands attention. Echeverría and his compatriots explored New Spain (now Mexico) and Central America on Spanish-chartered botanical expeditions in the late 1700s, brilliantly illustrating hundreds of plant and animal species previously unknown in the Old World. These collection voyages introduced the richness of the flora and fauna found in Mexico, where the greatest concentration of echeveria and agave reign, to the rest of the world.

Most members of this genus grow natively on stony cliff faces in higher elevations with moderately warm temperatures and low humidity. Rocky soils offer them excellent drainage, temperature modulation, and root-anchoring stability. The surrounding boulders provide thermal mass, heating up gradually during the day and releasing heat slowly in the evening. Using boulders or cobbles to minimize temperature extremes in your own garden is not only a great strategy for soothing your succulents, but stones can also be used to create a natural-looking design.

In cultivation, hens and chicks will reward you with robust growth in areas of full sun with good drainage, moderate temperatures, and sufficient airflow. With adequate sunshine throughout the day, plants will develop strong forms, vibrant colors, and disease resistance. Most hens and chicks are not shade-tolerant, and larger plants will stretch their stems (etiolate) quickly to reach more rays, eventually toppling over. More compact varieties tolerate some shade, but without a half day of sunlight, they won't exhibit the saturated color and shapely leaves that make them so desirable. If you are gardening in particularly hot climates, plants can benefit from a break from the strong afternoon sun.

Hens and chicks are fairly adaptable succulents that tolerate warm temperatures far better that the cold. Provided they have good drainage, most species will weather a light frost in the winter, but they will collapse and melt like the Wicked Witch of the West from *The Wizard of Oz* if they get too cold. The one exception with superior cold tolerance is the lipstick echeveria (*E. agavoides*). This geometric beauty resembles a dwarf agave with waxy, red-tipped leaves and is hardy to 15°F. Pictured on page 48 is a much sought after selection of *Echeveria agavoides* named 'Ebony', which sports especially deep maroon markings on its light green leaves.

In Coastal California, echeverias grow actively year-round. In warmer inland climates and areas with warmer temperatures, outer leaves can look a little crispy

OPPOSITE, TOP TO BOTTOM, LEFT TO RIGHT: *Graptoveria* 'Fred Ives', *Echeveria colorata* 'Mexican Giant', *Echeveria* 'Etna', *Echeveria* 'Dick Wright', Mexican snowball (*Echeveria elegans*), *Echeveria* 'Blue Curls', *Echeveria* 'Doris Taylor', *Echeveria* 'Afterglow', *Echeveria* 'Latte Rose'

in the heat of the summer, but they will return to their graceful beauty from fall through spring. A deep watering weekly to every few weeks is all that is needed to maintain plump growth and good color. Be careful with regular watering in the summer, however, especially in higher temperatures (90s to 100s F) or if plants are in heavy, slow-draining soils. Soggy, warm conditions encourage soil pathogens to proliferate and cause plant disease and loss. Roots should approach dryness between waterings, as they would in their natural habitat. As goes for all succulents, deep and infrequent watering is ideal.

After the plants have been in the ground for a year or two, you can experiment with restricting water. Look for puckering or shriveling leaves, which indicate that plants are thirsty. Remember that these plants, like camels, have adapted to extended periods without water. Some environmental stress is beneficial and will challenge roots to seek water deeper in the soil, creating even more drought tolerance for the future.

Cultivating hens and chicks in containers is almost as easy as growing the plants in ground. Most are great colonizers and will pup (produce offsets; see photo on this page) at the base, with new rosettes that spill over a pot's edge, creating the effect of a bouquet of roses. Pots should contain well-draining potting soil with sufficient nutrients and adequate room for root expansion.

Because most soft succulents are shallow rooted, containers don't need to be deep, but their width is important. Although packing an echeveria into a small container might look cute, the plant will fill up the pot with roots and consume soil nutrients fairly quickly and will need to be repotted.

Only a handful of succulents fare well indoors long term, while echeverias and many others tend to falter; pests, especially mealybugs, seem to appear spontaneously with the shortest stint of stagnant air. Mealybugs are a first

responder, indicating that drainage, air circulation, and/or sunlight are suboptimal. Overly moist potting soil or a location without good airflow invites pests to take up residence in cozy quarters.

Hens and chicks are the darlings of succulent collectors, and there are literally hundreds of attractive species and hybrids available. Many lovely boutique varieties grow well in curated greenhouse settings, but they won't pass muster in actual outdoor landscape conditions. In my experience growing echeverias outdoors in Coastal California, a few stand out from the rest in both beauty and durability.

Mexican snowball (*E. elegans*) and blue rose echeveria (*E.* x 'Imbricata') both produce generous amounts of suckers and form elegant silver and bluish carpets of 3- to 6-inch rosettes with delicate pink flowers. Lipstick echeveria (*E. agavoides*), the most cold-hardy species, features especially vivid foliage in the dark-tipped cultivars 'Lipstick' and 'Ebony'. *Echeveria* 'Afterglow' is luscious, with smoky pastel foliage that lingers somewhere between the colors of rose and lilac, depending on the light. A large cultivar, 'Afterglow' stands up well in full sun, forming impressive 2- to 3-foot colonies when mature.

The projects on pages 54–57 are a guide to incorporating these succulent gems into your landscape.

LEFT: Mexican snowball (*Echeveria elegans*)

RIGHT: *Echeveria* 'Ebony'

Pinwheel Hearts

A MEXICAN SNOWBALL
(*Echeveria elegans*)

There is nothing more rewarding than the living sequences that are set into motion by your own hands, and that grow into something beyond all expectations. Such is the case with this succulent-laden symbol of love. Surprisingly simple, a pinwheel heart warms garden nooks and planters alike. You can, with minor pruning and arranging, create a pinwheel heart using echeverias, aeonium—such as green platters (*Aeonium* 'Pseudotabuliforme'), other rosette-shaped succulents, or a mix.

This pinwheel heart requires a space of about 18 to 24 inches tall and wide. This is a good size to start with, or you can create a heart of any dimension using more or fewer plants.

Amend the soil with 2 to 6 inches of well-finished compost (see pages 134–37).

Visualize the heart shape or optionally, mark the shape with a line in the dirt, small stones, or thin metal, such as a wine-barrel hoop, bent into a heart shape to use as a template.

Insert a single Mexican snowball (from a 4-inch or 1-gallon container) into the center of the heart shape. This plant will produce more plants to fill the 18- to 24-inch space in 6 to 12 months. Or insert three or four smaller plants spread 6 inches apart for quicker results.

Water once or twice a week for 6 to 12 months or until the plants are established and rooted. As plants start to produce pups, or offsets, direct or prune them into the desired heart shape and size. If pups are filling the space unevenly or growing outside the perimeter, replant them to fill open spaces. The replanted pups will root and resume growth.

At six to twelve months, the heart will be full of rosettes and beaming with all the love you put into it. Once the heart has reached its desired size, remove any plants growing beyond the edges and share the love by planting another heart in a friend's garden.

Echeveria Jewel Box

A CUBIC FROST ECHEVERIA
(*Echeveria* 'Cubic Frost')

B RED FRILLS ECHEVERIA
(*Echeveria* 'Mauna Loa')

C WHITE CLOUD ECHEVERIA
(*Echeveria cante*)

D MEXICAN SNOWBALL
(*Echeveria elegans*)

E LATTE ROSE ECHEVERIA
(*Echeveria* 'Latte Rose')

F AFTERGLOW ESCHEVERIA
(*Echeveria* 'Afterglow')

Echeverias can create great synergy when they're mixed with other species, but this project concentrates several *Echeveria* species and cultivars together for an exclusive jam session. Luscious rosettes of overlapping leaves in silver, turquoise, amethyst, and pastel colors harmonize perfectly in horticultural concert. Layer them in a vignette with rocks, chunks of glass, driftwood, and other curiosities to make the most of their precious essences and differences in character.

Echeverias are low-growers, at 3 to 18 inches tall. To make the most visual impact, choose a spot on a natural slope or plant in a berm to provide the best viewing angle. This planted jewel box spans 12 by 15 feet, but you can scale the arrangement to any size you like.

If you're planting this vignette within a larger garden, create a border around a 12-by-15 foot space out of 4- to 8-inch cobbles or irregular-sized rock. The rock edging keeps the finished gravel top dressing separate from the surrounding mulch. Amend the soil with 2 to 6 inches of well-finished compost (see pages 134–37).

Create planting pockets within the larger space by adding small boulders to break up the space into smaller areas. Use twelve small (12 to 18 inches) boulders in clusters of three or four to form this effect. Sink rocks into the soil up to about third of their height to make them appear more natural—they should not be sitting on the surface.

Position the larger Cubic Frost echeveria, red frills echeveria, and white cloud echeveria toward the back of the area, and place several Mexican snowballs in the front, to anchor the edges and provide a "silver lining" to the space.

Group medium-sized Latte Rose and Afterglow echeverias centrally in clusters of three to seven plants depending on scale. Small groups of plants can be clustered around boulders or chunks of slag glass for an organic effect.

Top dress the area with 2 to 3 inches of $3/8$-inch gravel. Highlight specific areas with beach-glass or colorful pebbles to provide more sparkle.

CHAPTER 4

Aloe, What's Your Name?

Growing up as a redheaded youngster in the Florida sun, I could never seem to remember to bring along the sunscreen. So after a day at the beach or after a friend's pool party, I ended up looking like a lobster. *Aloe vera* came to the rescue, the gel from its leaves soothing my burnt skin. Little did I know that it was my introduction to one of the miracles of succulent plants.

In contrast to the panacea of its therapeutic uses, *A. vera* has quite the unsuspecting appearance. Lightly spotted leaves vary in color from gray to green, depending on the amount of sunlight they receive. The plant is fairly bombproof when grown indoors—which partially explains its global range and abundance. It will tolerate part shade, stale air, and leftover coffee for hydration. Happily pupping (producing offsets) to form a colony, this aloe's divisions are readily available and easily passed down through generations, like folklore. Outside in frost-free zones, it grows fairly fast in dense clusters of gray-green leaves that lose most of their stippling in full sun.

Sometimes called the lily of the desert, this humble aloe's use as an effective treatment of wounds and burns goes back 6,000 years to ancient Egypt and Greece, making it one of the earliest documented medicinal plants.

It's for good reason that we give *A. vera* the kudos it deserves and recognize it as being one of the most recognizable succulents in the world. But what about the other lesser-known 600-plus species in the *Aloe* genus? Surprisingly, many of the expansive species in the *Aloe* genus have lurked in relative obscurity from the gardening community and even the landscape trade for decades without great reason. Aloes have so many wonderful attributes that would top most gardeners' wish lists: They tolerate long periods without much water or attention; they provide a designer's treasure chest of leaf and flower colors, forms, and textures; and they offer a diversity of sizes to fit any micro- or macro-sized spaces. In addition, because of their soft marginal teeth and flexible leaves, aloes play well with other plants, pets, and people. It's hard to believe this garden-worthy palette of succulents has escaped our attention for so long.

Aloe marlothii hybrid

Lucky for us dirt-mongers, the succulent tide has been changing thanks to a merry band of horticulturists from The Huntington Botanical Gardens and a few other valiant aloe enthusiasts who have made it their mission to bring this underappreciated genus proper exposure. Intrepid breeders such as John Bleck in Santa Barbara, Kelly Griffin in San Diego, and Leo Thamm from Sunbird Aloes in South Africa have been pioneering more disease-resistant and compact garden aloes for decades. The fruits of their labors have ripened, making available many more unusual species and heavier blooming hybrid aloes. This is indeed good news for Mediterranean and arid climate gardeners, or even those in snowy climates with a greenhouse or pots that can be moved indoors for the winter.

Blooming mountain aloe (*Aloe marlothii*; yellow) and Zimbabwe aloe (*Aloe excelsa*; red)

Old World Beauties

Aloes are primarily African in origin, most hailing from the coastally influenced southern and eastern parts of the continent. Some species extend into the arid Arabian Peninsula and the volcanic islands of Madagascar and the Mascarenes. These rocky, rough, and dry regions have produced aloes that are genetically hardwired for endurance, making them winners in unforgiving conditions.

There are 300 unique species of aloe native to South Africa and Madagascar. South Africa, in particular, is a gardener's goldmine for distinctive plants, with the Cape Floristic Region holding the greatest density of species outside of the tropics. In particular, Table Mountain, a flat-topped mountain overlooking Cape Town, is home to more plant species than the entire United Kingdom. With so many species and hybrids of aloes now available, it can be difficult to choose only a few for your garden; this chapter focuses on the most garden-worthy aloe varieties.

Unpacking the Aloe Family

The varied architecture of *Aloe* species is full of great forms to experiment with in gardens of all sizes. From cartoonlike trees that only Dr. Seuss could dream up, to miniatures well suited for containers, many aloes are ready to enliven any landscape. Aloes can be arbitrarily split into three common forms—tree types, single-trunk, and clustering. Tree types are the largest and most captivating of the bunch, commonly reaching 8 to 30 feet at maturity. Single-trunk species are midsized plants that begin life as a chunky rosette and develop a single main stalk in time. Clustering aloes inhabit the lowest profile, forming 4- to 6-foot-wide colonies of rosettes that resemble a succulent shrub. That said, the many hybrids that can result from their promiscuous pollen create a variety of forms (a tree aloe can easily cross with a clustering aloe, for example). Books devoted specifically to aloes often divide the genus into as many as ten forms.

Beautiful pink, orange, and red colorations can appear in aloes when they receive strong heat, sun, or cold exposure.

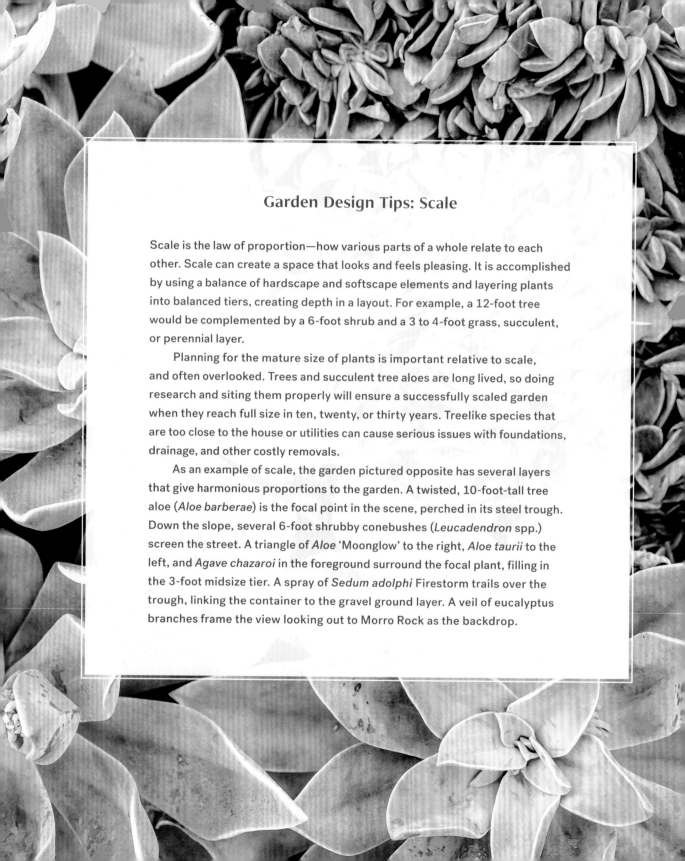

Garden Design Tips: Scale

Scale is the law of proportion—how various parts of a whole relate to each other. Scale can create a space that looks and feels pleasing. It is accomplished by using a balance of hardscape and softscape elements and layering plants into balanced tiers, creating depth in a layout. For example, a 12-foot tree would be complemented by a 6-foot shrub and a 3 to 4-foot grass, succulent, or perennial layer.

Planning for the mature size of plants is important relative to scale, and often overlooked. Trees and succulent tree aloes are long lived, so doing research and siting them properly will ensure a successfully scaled garden when they reach full size in ten, twenty, or thirty years. Treelike species that are too close to the house or utilities can cause serious issues with foundations, drainage, and other costly removals.

As an example of scale, the garden pictured opposite has several layers that give harmonious proportions to the garden. A twisted, 10-foot-tall tree aloe (*Aloe barberae*) is the focal point in the scene, perched in its steel trough. Down the slope, several 6-foot shrubby conebushes (*Leucadendron* spp.) screen the street. A triangle of *Aloe* 'Moonglow' to the right, *Aloe taurii* to the left, and *Agave chazaroi* in the foreground surround the focal plant, filling in the 3-foot midsize tier. A spray of *Sedum adolphi* Firestorm trails over the trough, linking the container to the gravel ground layer. A veil of eucalyptus branches frame the view looking out to Morro Rock as the backdrop.

TOWERING TITANS: THE TREE ALOES

Most of us think of trees as tall, woody, leafy plants that grow in forests, and succulents as desert ground-dwellers that don't grow over our heads. This small worldview of succulents is somewhat correct, with the exception of a few desert regions in the Americas and Africa that have the right climate for producing treelike species.

Aloe trees differ from more common conifers or hardwoods in that they feature larger trunk girths and canopy widths over vertical heights. Trunking aloes with dinosaur proportions have rightly earned such names as giant tree aloe (*Aloe barberae*, aka *Aloidendron barberae*), Mozambique tree aloe (*Aloe tongaensis*, aka *Aloidendron tongaensis*), and quiver tree (*Aloe dichotoma*, aka *Aloidendron dichotoma*), to name a few. These and other caudiciform aloes are recognizable by their swollen, bulbous, cartoonlike stems. South Africa is the source for all of the four stunning tree aloes profiled on pages 64–68.

One note of caution when planting these majestic, long-lived plants: Be wise and consider their ultimate size! For any tree aloe species, provide plenty of room away from roof overhangs, utilities, and permanent structures so their full stature can be appreciated without future issues.

Giant tree aloe

(*Aloe barberae*, aka *Aloidendron barberae*)

The giant tree aloe is widely distributed throughout the coastal forests of southeastern South Africa, which receives rainfall only in the summer. This is the most massive tree aloe of the family, growing to 60 feet tall in the wild, with an elephantine trunk. Over its lifetime, its pale-hued, bulbous trunk becomes its best feature. Its surface texture is smooth when young, morphing into a scaly, reptilian-like skin in adolescence. As the trunk expands, its upper branches fork out generously to form a canopy of rosettes, each branch having a spiky spray of foliage at the tips. The long leaves are dark green, arched, and deeply channeled. For such a statuesque plant, this aloe has relatively small racemes (clusters) of rose to salmon-colored flowers that peek through the foliage in late winter.

This easy, fast-growing species shows tolerance of both heavy and well-drained soils. Native to a summer-rainfall habitat, it will grow with extra vigor in regularly

Giant tree aloe (*Aloe barberae*) with author.

watered gardens but will readily adapt to dry conditions. A fantastic statement plant in the garden for its wow factor, its large, dark green canopy creates a buffered environment underneath for plants that prefer less intense rays, such as ox tongues (*Gasteria* spp.), aeoniums, and snake plants (*Sansevieria* spp.). The giant tree aloe is a favorite hangout for finches and other small birds in my garden, as the canopy provides plenty of protection. Give this impressive specimen a choice spot and plenty of elbow room, because it regularly grows to 20 to 30 feet in cultivation.

Mozambique tree aloe

(*Aloe tongaensis*, aka *Aloidendron tongaensis*)

In the northern reaches of its range in Zululand and southern Mozambique, the tree aloe diverges into a sister species—the smaller, low-branched Mozambique tree aloe (*A. tongaensis*). Known for its wild, snakelike branching, this tree aloe, at 6 to 12 feet, is a better fit for smaller spaces and still offers the characteristics of a tree aloe in a tighter package. Its presence is amplified when several are planted in the landscape. These aloes can be effectively staged as living sculptures flanking an entryway or planted in oversized containers.

Even when young, the Mozambique tree aloe has an open, multibranched habit, so its looser, Medusa-like presence is easy to distinguish from the stockier single-trunked form of the giant tree aloe. The Mozambique aloe's yellow and orange bicolored flowers stand proudly compared to the shy salmon-colored inflorescence of the giant aloe, which barely rise above the foliage. This aloe grows happiest in mild climates with minimal frost.

Quiver tree

(Aloe dichotoma, aka *Aloidendron dichotoma)*

Gardeners in more extreme winter and summer climates can consider this hardier giant of the western deserts of South Africa and Namibia. The quiver tree is a sun worshiper that inhabits rocky terrain that's baking hot and dry as a chip. Resenting most cool, foggy, maritime climates, quiver trees need heat and infrequent water to flourish. Naturally long lived, slow growing, and somewhat rare, they are a trophy in a good succulent collection.

The quiver tree is the most iconic of the desert aloes, forming concentrated stands in arid areas of Africa's Namaqualand. These aloes have a distinct shape, with a dense arrangement of smooth-skinned branches and leaves that resemble roots growing upside down. The golden brown bark develops large, scaly plates with age, with prominent ridges and valleys. The corky trunk tapers strongly from the base, with branches starting about halfway up. Rounded, canary-yellow flowers bloom in the summer on short stalks. After each bloom, new growth forks, or dichotomizes, to create its signature tightly branched canopy. The captivating presence of these trees en masse is difficult to describe and can be like a religious experience. To encounter their majesty firsthand, you can visit the Quiver Tree Forest in southern Namibia, where about 250 ancient specimens have held court for the last two or three centuries.

Fan aloe

(*Aloe plicatilis*)

Among a sea of wild and sometimes unruly species, the fan aloe (*A. plicatilis*) brings a sense of calm with its smooth, glaucous foliage. This attractive aloe is perhaps the friendliest of all *Aloe* species, with a soft, strappy form unique to the genus. It grows densely when young, hiding its single trunk, as juvenile leaves drop and its stout, grayish trunk branches and becomes exposed to resemble a bonsai in form. In cultivation, this aloe commonly reaches 4 to 6 feet, with some ancient specimens in nature reaching 20 or more feet and stretching 12 feet wide.

Its most striking feature is its wide, blue-green leaves that are flattened and stacked together at the branch ends, forming menorah-like shapes.

The fan aloe, along with plants of the family Proteaceae (Protea) and other scrub flora, grows in steep, sandy zones of the Fynbos region of South Africa, where it receives much annual rainfall (40 to 50 inches). It tolerates light frost, so site accordingly in colder winter regions. Partial afternoon shade is preferable in hot climates, with summer watering to prevent leaf burn.

In spring, fiery colored stalks of large, tubular flowers shoot up to the delight of hummingbirds. Unlike many aloes that bloom in tight clusters, the fan aloe's racemes are spaciously arranged on a tall stalk, revealing contrasting pale yellow interiors. This gentle and attractive aloe is one any gardener could love, and its soft form mixes well with arrangements of Mexican heather (*Cuphea* spp.), pearl bluebush (*Maireana sedifolia*), members of the Proteaceae family, Jerusalem sage (*Phlomis* spp.), and other Mediterranean natives.

OPPOSITE, TOP TO BOTTOM, LEFT TO RIGHT: *Aloe spicata, Aloe eximia, Aloe elegans* 'Yellow', *Aloe wickensii,* tilt-head aloe (*Aloe speciosa*), bitter aloe (*Aloe ferox*), Dwala aloe (*Aloe chabaudii*), *Aloe capitata, Aloe marlothii* x *excelsa*

THE SINGLE-TRUNK ALOES

In contrast to the branching form of tree aloes, these aloes maintain a single trunk (solitary) throughout their lives, with large crowns of leaves at their apex. Single-trunk species provide slender exclamations in the garden, similar in profile to a dwarf palm tree. These aloes include the most extraordinary bloomers of the tribe, so site them where the floral festivities can be easily appreciated.

Mountain aloe
(Aloe marlothii)

The mountain aloe (pictured opposite, left) is a robust, solitary-growing species native to the peaks, ridges, and buttes of the Western Cape of South Africa. From a chunky rosette of light green to bluish gray leaves in youth, its stout trunk begins to develop after three years. As the rosette gains elevation and lower leaves expire, they form a stiff, dried skirt around the trunk, protecting it from predation and sunburn. In its native habitat, the mountain aloe can grow to 12 feet tall, but 6 to 10 feet is more common in cultivation. Its foliage is more fully armed than most aloes, being studded with short, maroon spines along the margins and randomly on both sides of the leaves. The light-toned foliage contrasts with the dark, stubby spines, adding a palpable intensity to its appearance.

The mountain aloe is best known for its toughness and show-stopping blooms. Once established, it can exist in coastal conditions without supplemental water, although in its native habitat, it does receive summer rainfall. Plants will grow quicker the first few years if watered occasionally in summer. In addition to being drought-tolerant, the mountain aloe is cold-hardy and will tolerate a deeper freeze, into the 20s F.

The blooms of a mature (five or more years) mountain aloe are quite impressive and regularly garner exclamations by passersby, who marvel at their fireworks. The bloom phenomenon starts in the fall as an inky, fist-shaped bud emerges from between leaves. As this primary bud expands, a group of scaly racemes unfurls into a pyramid-shaped display. The ebony-colored stalk of the inflorescence branches wide, with individual arms angled horizontally. Hundreds of nectar-rich buds are packed on each raceme, gaining color as they swell into cigar-shaped flowers in tones of oranges, reds, and yellows. This aloe's strong presence can be appreciated from a distance, so positioning it 5 to 10 feet off a pathway will give it room to spread out but still be viewable in bloom.

With a wide variation of leaf and bloom colors across its native range, this species proudly shows off its distinctive characteristics. The red mountain aloe

(*A. marlothii* "Utrecht form") features brilliant, cherry-red flowers. When the mountain aloe crosses territory with close cousin bitter aloe (*A. ferox*), offspring can produce gorgeous ivory-colored and pale-yellow forms.

Tilt-head aloe

(*Aloe speciosa*)

This handsome species (pictured above, right) is more graceful and a bit less intimidating than the prickly mountain aloe, but it has an equally stunning bloom. With smooth, unarmed leaves up to 36 inches long, its rosette slants toward the strongest sunlight, for a pinwheel appearance. The large crown of pink-margined, glaucous foliage most commonly adorns a single trunk, 8 to 12 feet tall at maturity, but it will occasionally break the rules and branch to display multiple heads. Like most single-trunk aloes, the old leaves persist on the trunk, forming a sinuous skirt unless removed.

Although the temperatures in its native zones rarely plummet below the 30s F, tilt-head aloes have been documented to be hardy into the mid-20s F. With some protection when young, this plant is definitely worth trying in a marginal climate zone.

The species name, *speciosa*, means showy in Latin, and the bloom does not disappoint. Young plants may form only a single flower cone on each stalk, while older specimens produce multiple inflorescences on a short stalk held tightly to the rosette. The bloom procession starts in spring, with a tall, scaly inflorescence. Individual buds are a strawberry color when young, maturing to pale green with white stripe, and contrasting burgundy stamens. As the bloom cone matures from the bottom up, the multicolor effect is pronounced, with deep red flowers lowest on the cone, whitish flowers in the central portion of the cone, and unopened pinkish buds up top. One of the later flowering large aloes, tilt-head aloe blooms light up the late winter garden and usher in the spring.

For a groomed appearance, remove the tattered leaf skirt to reveal the woody trunk underneath. If you prefer the looks of the unpruned leaf skirt around the trunk, add plants such as low-growing spider flowers (*Grevillea lanigera* 'Coastal Gem') or *G.* 'Magic Lantern', or the long-blooming Mexican lobelia (*Lobelia laxiflora*) perennial to echo the aloe's reddish highlights.

To view a planting of impressive mature tilt-head aloes, make a pilgrimage to the Desert Garden at The Huntington Botanical Gardens in San Marino, California, or to Lotusland in Montecito, California, where the Blue Garden was renovated in 2012 to reflect opera singer and gardener Ganna Walska's original design of the 1950s.

THE CLUSTERING ALOES

Clustering aloes are shrubby in nature. Although the words "shrub" and "shrubby" can seem boring terms that usually refer to a drab group of hedging and parking lot plants, these terms can be used to describe a more pleasing stature with regard to aloes whose spreading growth habit offers a dense structure. Here are a few choice aloes that are clustering in posture.

Sunset aloe
(*Aloe dorotheae*)

Most aloes, such as the tilt-head and mountain aloes, are known for their impressive cool-season blooms, and other species, such as the fan aloe and sunset aloe (pictured opposite, left), shine year-round as foliage superstars. Sunset aloe, in particular, has the most wildly colored foliage, which morphs between tones of burnt orange, red, coral, and lime green. Even if this aloe never bloomed, it would still top lists for its psychedelic color palette.

Shaped like ribbed daggers, short and triangular with abbreviated points along the margins, the glossy foliage forms whorls around the suckering stems in a spiral arrangement. When grown in intense sunlight with little water, the sunset aloe's foliage will change in color from green, to coral-orange, to fire-engine red, to a dark crimson hue. The center of the rosette remains lime green as the outer leaves move through the seasonal color wheel.

This ground-hugger rarely grows taller than 18 inches, with a 2- to 3-foot spread, making it a perfect plant for the front of the border. When plants are clustered among rocks, they give the effect of glazed starfish on the ocean floor. The leaves' waxy sheen gives the plant an almost plastic look that must be touched to be believed.

A great candidate for the mixed garden, this aloe blends well with water-wise perennials such as Spanish needles (*Bidens* spp.), shrubby primrose (*Calylophus* spp.), and *Isoplexis* spp. within the foxglove family, as well as warm-toned Coppertone stonecrop (*Sedum nussbaumerianum* 'Coppertone'; see page 31) and ice plants (such as *Delosperma* 'Fire Spinner'). For additional low-growing border highlights, check out the summer- and fall-blooming *Aloe* 'Cynthia Giddy' and *A.* 'Rooikappie'.

In the midst of positive attributes, the only asset the sunset aloe lacks is cold-hardiness; it sustains damage in frosty temperatures. In conditions similar to those of its native habitat in Tanzania, East Africa, this aloe will be happiest in full sun with mild winter temperatures above 30°F.

Coral aloe

(*Aloe striata*)

Moving up the height scale for clustering types, coral aloe (pictured above, right) is a vibrant crowd-pleaser. This medium-sized aloe is widely adaptable, being frost-tolerant and unfussy about soil types, making it a rewarding plant for beginners. As with many other aloes, its foliage reacts to the sun's intensity; in part shade, its foliage is a celadon green color, and in full sun, foliage exhibits a brilliant aqua color with pastel or peachy flushes. The spineless leaves are accented by a bold coral-colored outline (darker in cool weather), with subtle white stripes running along their length.

Coral aloes start out as single rosettes and will cluster out to form colonies up to 4 to 5 feet at maturity. A marvelous winter bloomer, its branched bloom stalks rise from each rosette, with large clusters of glowing orange flowers that unfurl in a candelabra shape. Hummingbirds and bees are magnetically drawn to these nectar-rich flowers, making this is a great plant for a wildlife-friendly garden. With its manageable size, the coral aloe can be positioned either front stage or centrally in the landscape, with its lively colors becoming more pronounced when groups of plants are used in the border. Interplanting coral aloe with coppertone stonecrop (*Sedum nussbaumerianum* 'Coppertone'; see page 31) and pink-hued echeverias will heighten the cheer, while pairing with sapphire-colored senecios or Blue Spruce stonecrop (*Sedum reflexum* 'Blue Spruce') brings a welcome contrast.

Van Balen's aloe
(*Aloe vanbalenii*)

The "undersea garden" is an inviting theme to explore with succulents, as many plants, such as this aloe, possess the fluid and crested forms of hard and soft corals undulating in the current. When planted alongside octopus aloe (*A. vilmoriniana*) and spider aloe (*A. bracteosa*), Van Balen's aloe can help you achieve the look.

This tightly clustered aloe appears stemless, but it will pup to form colonies of about 2 feet tall and 5 feet wide when provided ample room. Deeply channeled, bright green leaves whimsically twist up and around, eventually brushing the ground with their tips. Blooming commences in the spring with tall, slender spikes of vivid orange or red buds opening to yellow or ivory-colored flowers, depending on the selection.

Native to summer rainfall areas in South Africa, it thrives with occasional water in the growing season, preferring to stay dry in winter. When plants are grown in strong sun with minimum water, the colors of the fine teeth along the leaf margins begin warming to orange tones, with the entire leaf surface eventually flushing to deep corals and reds in response to stress.

Its curious shape lends Van Balen's aloe to a prominent place in the border, where its limbs can unfurl and be appreciated. Its short stature is a plus in a border planting, where it can be placed in the foreground and won't obscure plants behind it. Consider planting grasses such as *Cordyline* 'Cha-Cha' or the rainbow-colored foliage of mirror bush (*Coprosma* spp.) as colorful companions.

If you're aiming to re-create a reef habitat, use this aloe as a focal point, and add some heat with clusters of coral-like fire sticks (*Euphorbia* 'Sticks on Fire') and sunset aloe (*Aloe dorotheae*). Cool it off with chalky senecios, cotyledons, and pastel echeverias. It also looks great staged in a container, with its octopus arms gracefully cascading over the edges of the pot. In addition, with a containerized plant, you'll find it easier to restrain from watering during the winter, which brings out its reddish leaf color.

Aloes in Wonderland

A BOTTLE TREE
(*Brachychiton rupestris*)

B MOUNTAIN ALOE
(*Aloe marlothii*)

C BREAD PALM
(*Encephalartos* spp.)

D BOTTLEBRUSH ALOE
(*Aloe rupestris*)

E ZIMBABWE ALOE
(*Aloe excelsa*)

F MAIDEN'S QUIVER TREE
(*Aloe ramosissima*)

Among cycads, cacti, caudiciforms, and many other rare oddities, Jeff Chemnick of Santa Barbara, California specializes in growing aloes. His five-acre habitat-style garden is a striking example of mass planting different varieties of the same genus.

In this vignette, open-shaped rosettes of silvery aloes and dark green cycads are the dominant players, with Madagascar ocotillo, MacDougall's century plant, and beaked yuccas fading into the background. A sculpture of a young pony centers the composition, providing visual relief to the jungle theater. This specific layout may be challenging to reproduce exactly, but you can use other species to create a similar naturalistic planting.

Amend the soil with 2 to 6 inches of well-finished compost (see pages 134–37).

When you're planning to plant densely over a large area, first establish one or more focal points for the eye to rest on. Using specimen plants or sculptures either alone or in small groupings visually anchors the space to give a sense of calm among the density. The horse statue and the bulbous trunk of the bottle tree serve this purpose in this project.

Next, choose a dominant plant, such as a mountain aloe, with its orange-yellow candelabra-shaped blooms, and plant several to weave like a river throughout the garden, creating movement and cohesion. Similar aloes to substitute for a smaller space could be Dwala aloe (*Aloe chabaudii*), red aloe (*A. cameronii*), or Blue Elf aloe (*A.* 'Blue Elf').

Throughout the area, plant repeating clusters of ferny green cycads such as bread palms to contrast the river of mountain aloe. Cycad foliage often has a waxy sheen, which provides a reflective quality as opposed to the matte surfaces of the aloes.

Dotted occasionally throughout the garden, plant other aloes including tall, dark green bottlebrush aloes; sprays of red-flowering Zimbabwe aloes; and short but densely branched maiden's quiver trees. Keep these accents to a minimum to add variety but not detract from the dominant plantings of mountain aloe and the contrasting silvery aloes and bread palms.

Moonlighting

A MARINA STRAWBERRY TREE
(*Arbutus* 'Marina')

B MOONGLOW ALOE
(*Aloe* 'Moonglow')

C ORANGE HOT POKER
(*Kniphofia* 'Shining Sceptre')

D SIERRA MIXTECA AGAVE
(*Agave oteroi* 'Felipe Otero')

E QUADRICOLOR CENTURY PLANT
(*Agave lophantha* 'Quadricolor')

F MOROCCAN MOUND
(*Euphorbia resinifera*)

This project incorporates a few strategies to transform a slender, flat front yard into a dynamic landscape. Concentrations of species are contrasted by looser, open areas of boulders and gravel. The repetition of strawberry trees and aloes provides a veil of privacy from the street, while open graveled pockets make the space feel larger. Contoured soil berms create a visually interesting topography and improve drainage capacity critical for succulents. The golden-blooming *Aloe* 'Moonglow' that knits together this composition is a hybrid developed by Leo Thamm of Sunbird Aloes. From his nursery in South Africa, Leo has been a front-runner in introducing very floriferous varieties on compact succulent plants. Since the majority of aloes, such as 'Moonglow', are winter-blooming, they provide an arresting surprise in the garden when many other plants are resting.

Starting with the berms, build two subtle mounds about 8 to 12 inches tall and 15 by 20 feet wide. These will roll toward a rocky, dry creek bed that you'll create. For the most natural appearance, berms should take a wide and gradual approach to elevation, rather than being short and steep like a volcano. You will need about 6 yards of compost or planting mix per berm. If you want to build smaller berms, use less soil.

Between the berms, build a dry creek bed from rounded stone cobbles to assist with drainage and define the planting space.

Place rust-colored, red granite rocks in small groupings of three to five throughout the space to provide structure, color, and contrast to the plants.

Between the berms and the house, plant two or three multitrunked strawberry trees to provide rich, green, screening canopies and to create privacy and scale to the area. Plant the trees about 20 to 30 feet apart, or far enough apart to offer selective views of the house from the garden and street.

Use Moonglow aloe as the anchor plant for the berms, with its dense clumps of slender blue foliage in the summer and an exquisite floral show in the winter. Space 3 plants 5 to 8 feet apart in the front half of the yard for street-side appeal. Intersperse 3 orange hot poker clumps in the midground between the aloes. The orange blooms of the hot poker plant appear in summer after the yellow spires of the Moonglow aloe are gone (the photo on page 78 was taken in winter), giving your garden color throughout the seasons.

Fill up the open space between the repeating aloes and orange pokers with a few compact specimens, such as the solitary Sierra Mixteca agave, whose leaf edges resemble thick parchment with large, recurved (backward-facing) teeth. Plant a variegated Quadricolor century plant to highlight a nearby rust-colored boulder in the foreground, and plant a Moroccan mound euphorbia near the front to form a low mound of tightly packed, grayish green columns.

Finish with a fine, $3/8$-inch neutral-colored gravel mulch layer, to contrast the various green tones and coarse textures of the plants.

Aloe 'Moonglow'

CHAPTER 5

The Spiny Side

Agave, yucca, and cacti represent the purest expression of the succulent ethos. They've adapted to the driest of climates with their ability to conserve water in multiple ways. Like all succulents, precious water is stored in the flesh of the plants, under a thick skin, but many spiny succulents undergo more frugal forms of photosynthesis, where respiration occurs only at night. This upgraded process keeps pores closed during the hot day to minimize water loss.

With their long lifespan, these plants undergo slow and measured growth. Nutritional sugars can be stored for years (or decades) in lean times, until conditions are best for blooming, when they are used to feed flower growth to provide seeds for the next generation. These succulents' conservancy and perseverance have inspired legions of gardeners to embrace a greater sense of environmental stewardship in their own landscapes. At their core, they represent a will to endure despite tough conditions. Each spine, trichome (fine hair), and toothed margin embodies a spirit of sovereignty.

That said, these drought-tolerant wonders don't require a dry, hot climate to thrive. By planting them in mounded soil for better drainage and placing them carefully in appropriate microclimates, gardeners in humid, wet, and cold climates can experience spiny success as well. Agaves in Alabama? Opuntia in Oregon? Yuccas in Wyoming? You bet! These are highly adaptable plants with underdog coded into their DNA.

Once the addiction to softer succulents peaks and your thirst isn't quenched by the latest lovely echeveria, you may find the urge to meet the tough guys across the tracks. This edgy band of botanical outcasts has a little more to prove to win your attention, but if your judgment can be tempered, these prickly beauties add new dimensions to the water-wise palette. This chapter focuses on plants that are fairly common to the trade, easy to cultivate, and are beautiful additions to any garden.

Compass barrel cactus (*Ferocactus cylindraceus*)

Agave

The agave's striking radial symmetry and sweeping distribution across arid zones of the Americas make it hard to miss. All agaves are "New World" plants (native to the Americas) and grow in a remarkable diversity of habitats, from sea level to 8,000 feet. They excel in arid and semi-arid climates, as well as temperate mixed forests, among shrubs and small trees. Agaves are known commonly as century plants for their propensity to take many years to bloom (usually ten to thirty years). After the plant blooms, its foliage desiccates and dies. However, many agaves readily produce pups (offsets) to succeed the mother plant as it expires.

Cultivated in the landscape, century plants have enjoyed a wonderful renaissance in the last decade, with plant collectors and breeders releasing a host of compact and colorful varieties for the everyday gardener. The ubiquitous American century plant, *A. americana*, has an unfortunate reputation as a spreader that suckers profusely, forming large and dense colonies. Recent breeding efforts have focused on bringing solitary or smaller clustering agaves to the market. Solitary plants produce only one main rosette, or occasionally a small number of pups, and are more manageable in the garden.

Many 6- to 10-foot agaves appear quite deadly because of the large, sharp spines on their leaf tips, and many residential plots are too small to accommodate plants of this size. Therefore, this discussion is limited to the best small to midsized garden-worthy plants.

SMALL AGAVES

For our purposes, a small agave ranges from 1 to 3 feet tall and wide. My favorites for style, size, and sophistication are Ocahui agave (*A. ocahui*), squid agave (*A. bracteosa*), twin-flowered agave (*A. geminiflora*), butterfly agave (*A. potatorum*), and Queen Victoria agave (*A. victoriae-reginae*).

Ocahui agave
(*Agave ocahui*)

Hailing from rocky hillsides up to 4,500 feet in the southwestern United States and the state of Sonora east of Baja California, Mexico, is the Ocahui (oh-KAH-hwee) agave (pictured opposite, left), which in the indigenous vernacular means cord or tongue. Its perfectly symmetrical, slender, forest-green leaves with toothless edges make it a true representation of organic architecture. This hardy species thrives in

heat but is cold-tolerant to at least 15°F. Even though small in size, its rigid, swordlike leaves require that it be placed deliberately; you don't want to topple over this plant.

Ocahui is an ideal candidate for a patio container, where its brilliance can be viewed up close. It requires only monthly water during the growing season. Ocahui has passed on its compact traits and cold tolerance to a few stellar hybrids, one of my favorites being *A*. 'Blue Glow' (see photos on pages 90 and 106), which forms a beautiful single rosette, with deep blue foliage highlighted by yellow and red margins.

Squid agave
(*Agave bracteosa*)

This oceanic-looking agave (pictured above, right) is one of the kindest century plants you'll meet. Clusters of olive-green foliage form an hourglass shape at the base and gracefully recurve toward the ground. Wavy foliage emerging from the crown dances with older leaves higher up, giving the plant a remarkable sense of movement, a rare treat in agaves.

In its native habitat, the Chihuahuan Desert of northern Mexico and the southwestern United States, this plant grows from vertical limestone bluffs at elevations up to 5,500 feet, sustaining cold tolerance down to 10°F.

A slow grower, it will form a respectable colony of pups in a favorable year. If you're not a fan of spines, this agave will become a favorite in your collection, being completely barb-free. Its ease of culture and figurative posture make it a standout specimen in a decorative container or in the ground. The cascading foliage looks especially artful when plants are installed on a raised berm or in a tall pot. Keep an eye out for the unusual white-banded selection, 'Monterrey Frost', shown in the image.

Twin-flowered agave
(*Agave geminiflora*)

The twin-flowered agave (pictured above, left) forms an even, round mass of flexible, dark green leaves. Each plant is composed of hundreds of smooth, spaghetti-wide leaves that radiate outward in relaxed symmetry. Because its pliable leaves lack terminal spines, this agave can be planted close to a walkway. In its native habitat in the state of Nayarit, in western Mexico, it prefers to grow in the light shade of a tree canopy or close to a seasonal creek bed. It looks best in the garden with supplemental water every few weeks, planted away from areas of extreme heat.

Butterfly agave
(*Agave potatorum*)

This chameleon (pictured above, center) displays a variable structure in its native habitat, from Puebla to Oaxaca and into Chiapas, Mexico. Its common name comes from the Náhuatl language spoken by indigenous Aztecs, who admired its symmetrical form and usefulness in fermenting mescal. Its typical habit is a solitary rosette with an open display of cupped, powder-blue leaves contrasted by reddish spines. A great subject for breeding, its crosses produce some choice selections in the nursery trade.

I would be remiss not to mention one last agave, an *Agave potatorum* variety called 'Kissho Kan' or 'Kichiokan marginata' (pictured above, right). "Kissho Kan" translates from Japanese into "happy crown." This variegated gem is a Japanese selection, slow growing and lesser known in the trade. Worth seeking out, this agave assumes a tightly stacked temple of upturned leaves, chalky blue in the center with wide, creamy yellow margins. Tiny stiff spines pinpoint the edges of the foliage, changing from golden to dark brown as they mature. It will form a few pups in time, while assuming its mature pagoda form within 4 to 5 years. At only 12 inches tall by 18 inches wide, this is a nearly perfect specimen to enjoy growing in any succulent garden.

Queen Victoria agave
(*Agave victoriae-reginae*)

The Queen Victoria agave honors the nineteenth-century English queen. Within its tight whorl of dark green foliage are individual leaves edged in streaks of brilliant white. At close inspection, each leaf is faceted into multiple planes like a cut diamond; a semi-mature specimen is a real showstopper.

This agave has a lot going for it, from high heat tolerance to laughing off freezing temperatures in the teens. When not overwatered, its slow, measured growth makes a longstanding companion in a gardener's journey. Give this agave four to five years to develop its signature sphere shape, as its irregular leaf layout during the juvenile stage tends to resemble a modern sputnik lamp. In garden cultivation, its golden flowers emerge at ten to twenty years, after which the plant dies. The Queen Victoria agave is mostly solitary in its native habitat, the Chihuahuan Desert, though some populations are known to produce a few pups.

Although this agave maintains a collector status, it is often more available in nurseries than other rare, though highly sought-after, species. Plant Queen Victoria agaves on a mound and/or provide excellent drainage, because they disdain wet feet, especially in winter. They are fantastic in a container as well. Strongly variegated selections are a bit less cold- and heat-tolerant, so be sure to install prized plants in suitable locations.

MIDSIZE AGAVES

Midsize agaves in the 3- to 6-foot range bring structure, drama, and focal points to the water-wise garden. Their scale captures attention from afar with a shapely architecture, but they won't overwhelm the space like some larger colonizing species.

Octopus agave

(*Agave vilmoriniana*)

The octopus agave has slender, spineless, curving arms that create an eye-catching, wondrous spectacle. Its fluid posture is distinct, with wavy leaves surging up and curling back toward the ground. Noted for forming extensive vertical colonies on its cliff-side terrain in the states of Durango and Jalisco, Mexico, this agave inspired pioneer American botanist and agave expert Howard Gentry to compare its appearance to giant spiders on a wall.

A fast grower in the cultivated landscape, the octopus agave reaches maturity in four to eight years, so plan for it being a garden highlight and not a long-term fixture like other agaves. Its asymmetrical artistry builds after the first few flushes of leaves have matured and more curvaceous tentacles emerge.

Being a solitary grower, the octopus agave produces no pups, but if the flower stalk is allowed to mature, it will generate hundreds of tiny bulbils or plantlets that are ready to root. When the bittersweet flowering stage does arrive, its 15- to 20-foot stalk is topped with canary-yellow flowers. The unbranched inflorescence elevates so quickly that you can notice daily growth in its skyward trajectory. Flowers are a fiesta for flocking bees and hummingbirds, so enjoy the party as they unfurl. Pictured opposite is a stunning variegated selection of the octopus agave named 'Stained Glass'.

Smooth agave

(*Agave desmetiana*)

Somewhere between the loose form of octopus agave and the compact varieties of *Agave potatorum* lies the beautiful species *Agave desmetiana*. Thought to be native to a region near Sinaloa, Mexico, this agave has been extensively cultivated in the nursery trade as an ornamental plant. The smooth agave has unique, deeply channeled leaves that emerge from the rosette in an attractive hourglass shape. The curvature of the leaves make them look flexible, though the foliage is surprisingly stiff. With mostly smooth leaf margins, this plant resides on the friendlier side of the agave cast, wielding only a terminal spine on each leaf to remind us of its request for personal space.

Smooth agaves reach around 3 feet tall and wide and offset prolifically. For an attractive profile, allow the mother rosette to gain a clean pineapple-shaped form and remove the side shoots during growth. Pups are a nice bonus to start the next generation after flowering commences; let them develop as the mother plant fades. Cold-tender in nature, this agave tolerates temperatures above 30°F, but it should be covered during frostier temperatures. Along coastlines with mild temperatures, it does well in full sun, but it benefits from afternoon shade in hotter climates.

Yucca

Yuccas are attractive, long-lived plants in the landscape with bold textures and beautiful blooms. Most yuccas hide their stout stems under layers of swordlike leaves, though many show off their trunks with bravado. Their sharp terminal leaf spines can prove painful if you encounter them while moving too quickly. Arborescent (treelike) species can have single trunks or many branches, such as the iconic Joshua tree (*Y. brevifolia*), which can reach 50 feet tall and 5 feet wide.

Yuccas are a smaller genus of succulents, with around fifty species, but they make up for their numbers in their adaptability to North America's diverse range of climates. Yuccas span the plains of Canada, traverse through the lower forty-eight states, and extend south into Central America and east to the Atlantic, plus a few islands in the Caribbean.

Banana yucca (*Y. baccata*), soapweed (*Y. glauca*), soaptree yucca (*Y. elata*), and weak-leaf yucca (*Y. flaccida*) hail from frigid USDA Zones 4 and 5 and make good choices for cold-climate gardens. These species are some of the most bombproof succulents and can shake off both searing desert sun and bone-chilling below-zero temperatures. If you think you can't grow succulents in the ice, try these alpine gems.

Speaking of hardiness, Bright Star yucca (*Y.* Bright Star) is a magnificent variegated selection that thrives in the heat and is cold-tolerant down to 10°F. Its swordlike leaves sport wide yellow margins that give the rosette a glowing appearance. This cultivar develops a short trunk in time, but keeps a compact form of 18 to 30 inches tall. Stunning spikes of pink buds open to white flowers in summer, making this cultivar a year-round focal point.

Most yuccas are polycarpic, meaning plants produce flowers and seeds many times after they mature, unlike agaves, which die after producing a flower spike. Although many yuccas can appear dangerous and attain stout proportions, the landscape-friendly varieties that follow are surefire winners for small to midsized gardens.

OPPOSITE, TOP TO BOTTOM, LEFT TO RIGHT: *Agave* 'Mr. Ripple', compass barrel cactus (*Ferocactus cylindraceus*), Moroccan mound (*Euphorbia resinifera*), thread agave (*Agave filifera*), *Agave* 'Blue Glow', blue candle (*Myrtillocactus geometrizans*), *Agave gentryi* 'Jaws', *Echinopsis huascha*, whale's tongue agave (*Agave ovatifolia*)

RIGHT: *Yucca* Bright Star

Red yucca

(*Hesperaloe parviflora*)

Botanists love to quarrel and reclassify species over time, which keeps gardeners on their toes. Plants of the genus *Hesperaloe*, for example, are sometimes labeled as *Hesperoyucca*. Slight differences in flowers and anatomical morphology, however, have cleaved species of the genus *Hesperoyucca* from the rest of the true yucca family.

Red yucca (pictured above, left), under any name, is a beautiful and rugged succulent worth growing. Also known as Texas yucca, this acaulescent (stemless) yucca resembles a reed or ornamental grass. From the Chihuahuan Desert, it loves full sun and is cold-hardy to Zone 5 (to –15°F). The highlight of the species is definitely the dramatic wandlike inflorescent blooms that are thrown skyward for half the year. At 4 to 8 feet tall, bright pink flower stalks emerge, with flowers ranging from coral-pink to radiant red in the cultivar Brakelights yucca. Petal interiors are brushed in a creamy white and sometimes yellow, offering a pleasing contrast. The grassy mass, at 3 to 5 feet wide and about 3 feet tall, appears forest-green from a distance, and its texture is best highlighted in groupings in the landscape.

Beaked yucca

(*Yucca rostrata*)

Arguably one of the most attractive water-wise landscape plants available, this slow-growing tree-form yucca (pictured opposite, middle) is unique for its nearly spherical crown of slender, silvery blue leaves. A few other yuccas have enchanting blue foliage, but none of them come close to the shimmering haze of the beaked yucca. Cold-hardy to USDA Zone 5 (to −15°F) and also heat-loving, this majestic species will last in the garden for decades.

Leaves have sharp points but are long and flexible with no marginal armor. Older foliage gracefully falls down the trunk in a natural grass skirt that protects the plant from sunburn. This skirt can be removed for a groomed appearance but looks handsome when intact.

The plant's native habitat includes dry, rocky slopes with excellent drainage, from south Texas to Mexico, so it performs best in warm, dry areas. In clay soils, install plants in a mound, and water very infrequently or not at all once plants are established. In late spring, large panicles of white flowers rocket upward. An architectural statement, plant beaked yucca to set off a main entry, or mass plants in groups for a stunning grove effect.

Weak-leaf yucca

(*Yucca flaccida*)

The weak-leaf yucca (pictured opposite, right) grows throughout the Appalachia region in the eastern United States and extends south to the humid Florida coast. In well-drained soil, this yucca is equally comfortable in a Pennsylvania winter or a Florida summer.

Leaves are pliable with a fuzzy texture and an abundance of scroll-like fibers that peel away from the plant. In attractive clumps, new foliage stands tall, as older leaves arch downward.

This species is regarded by some taxonomists as a form of *Y. filamentosa*, which is fairly similar in stature, and the two species names can be used interchangeably in the marketplace. Two variegated cultivars, *Y. filamentosa* 'Color Guard' and *Y. flaccida* 'Golden Sword', light up the succulent or mixed perennial garden throughout the year. These lax-leaved varieties are radiant, with widely banded, golden foliage that provides a glowing appearance more yellow than green.

Cacti: Columns, Paddles, and Barrels

Many archetypes are associated with the strange, mostly leafless, spiny, and swollen-stemmed cacti. Their extraterrestrial shapes are icons in John Wayne westerns, go hand-in-hand with desert legends, and epitomize the will to survive.

Cacti are both simple in nature and grossly misunderstood. They continually straddle a line of duality, being beautiful and barbaric, aggressive and silent, peculiar and pedestrian. Based on these strong subjective impressions, our culture has developed a staunch polarity in how we regard cacti as friend or foe, scourge or sculpture. In any case, members of the persistent Cactaceae family have outlasted the pretense placed upon them to share their truth—if we can hear what they have to say.

Cacti are the plant kingdom's "special ops" that can tackle the toughest habitats on Earth. They are a testament to biological perseverance. Cacti present a compilation of highly modified features, packaged ingeniously to withstand the most inhospitable environments, from the tropical Americas to Africa and South America, to the highest elevations from Canada to Patagonia.

As explained on page 2, all cacti are succulents, but not all succulents are cacti. What separates cacti from other succulents is the presence of areoles. These cushiony structures can be either raised or sunken on the plant surface and are often covered with a micropuff of fine hairs. Areoles are the main evolutionary modifications that enable cacti to streamline their anatomy, with no leaves and branches—only plump stems. Areoles have varying layouts that respond closely to environmental cues of climate and predation. In barrel cacti, they are dense and distributed evenly along a plant's ribs, with straight or curved spines completely preventing access to the plant's trunk. In some cacti, such as the common Christmas cactus (genus *Schlumbergera*) areoles are concentrated

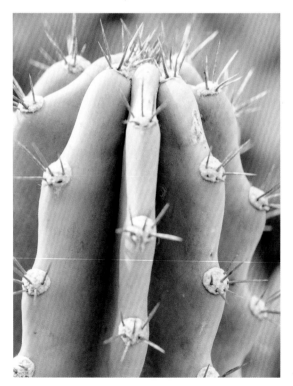

White cushion-like areoles on monstrose apple cactus (*Cereus peruvianus* f. *monstrose*).

at the ends of stems and present not for protection, but for producing the prized and colorful holiday flowers.

The family Cactaceae is fairly large and diverse, numbering 1,500 to 1,800 species, depending on who's counting. To avoid getting too deep in a taxonomic quagmire, I'll keep it simple by classifying its members by their distinct growth habits.

COLUMNAR CACTI

The most ubiquitous symbol of the dry country, columnar cacti are indelibly etched into our collective minds by gift shop postcards, buckaroo paraphernalia, and cartoonish silhouettes with arms akimbo.

The grand saguaro (sah-WAH-roh) cactus (*Carnegiea gigantea*) typifies the columnar form and is widespread across the Sonoran Desert in Arizona and Mexico, and areas of Southern California. As old and wise as the venerable oak tree, wild saguaro cacti have been recorded in heights of up to 78 feet tall, and three centuries old. One of the oldest champions, an Oro Valley, Arizona, saguaro aptly named Granddaddy, had more than fifty-two arms and reached 40 feet tall by the time it collapsed in 1992. Growth ekes along for saguaros in desert conditions, where it takes nearly ten years to achieve its first inch, thirty years to produce its first flowers, and around sixty years to amass enough energy to extend its first arm. The saguaro's faster growing cousin, the giant cardon (*Pachycereus pringlei*; pictured on page 96), looks very similar and doesn't take generations to mature.

One of the most prominent evolutionary features exemplified in the columnar cactus are the heavy ribs that punctuate the exterior skin. Looking at a cross-section of a stem, the deeply pleated shape resembles an accordion and is able to expand and contract in good or lean water times. As the spongy tissue inside the cactus absorbs water, the plant's skin balloons out, creating further holding capacity. Cacti root systems are fairly shallow, spreading mostly in the top 3 to 6 inches of earth in order to gather surface water from fast-moving summer monsoon rains. The bladderlike system inside a large cactus can hold up to a ton of water, creating a sustaining reservoir to savor for extended periods.

Columnar cacti grow more quickly in garden conditions. Like a specimen Japanese or paperbark maple that requires ten to twenty years to develop its form, a columnar cactus is a slow and steady investment you can bank on as an eventual visual centerpiece, not to mention a family heirloom. When established, they require strong sun and well-drained soil, period. The list of what they need is much shorter than what they can do without. In fact, caring for them in the garden takes some

adjustment on the gardener's part and is a good exercise in restraint. They do need occasional water during the first couple years to establish a good root system. Beyond that, however, minimal care is required, with only occasional grooming to maintain their sharp looks.

Cacti from Mexico, such as giant cardon (*Pachycereus pringlei*), organ pipe cactus (genus *Stenocereus*), blue-skinned cacti (genus *Pilosocereus*), or old man cactus (genus *Cephalocereus*), are tolerant of heat but not so much the cold. If your winters bring light frost, they'll need protection from the chill and/or placement in a microclimate close to the house or another appropriate area. On the other end of the climate spectrum, mountain-growing species from South America, such as San Pedro cacti (*Echinopsis pachanoi*) or silver torch cacti (*Cleistocactus strausii*), abide temperatures in the 20s F and are able to tolerate a much wider range of cultivation possibilities. The two species highlighted here are good beginner specimens that can handle a bit of both sides.

OPPOSITE: Cardon cactus (*Pachycereus pringlei*) beginning to branch out.

Old man of Mexico cactus

(*Cephalocereus senilis*)

Some plants' names are as quirky as the people who collect them. This one has earned many nicknames, including old man of Mexico, old man cactus, and *viejo* (Spanish for old) cactus, because of its shaggy, long, white, beardlike hairs that obscure small spines on the stem. This is a beautiful, slow-growing species in cultivation, approaching a manageable 6 to 8 feet tall in its first decade. Older cacti have been known to stretch to more than 20 feet tall in the wilds of Hidalgo and Veracruz, Mexico. The endearing beard, which thins as the cactus ages, makes for great contrast in the mixed dry garden. This species isn't freeze-hardy like its other senior cousins, so it's best in low-desert gardens in a frost-free area, where this easy cactus fares well in a patio container. Or grow it as a house plant by a sunny window.

Handling Spiny Specimens

Although working bare-handed with cacti can be treacherous, you can safely move and plant them by taking a few precautions. All cactus spines look stiff, but most are pliable and resistant to breakage (or puncturing you) when handling if you protect them and yourself. Most spines won't regrow once broken, so plan your choreography and move slowly and carefully as if performing tai chi!

1. Prepare the planting hole (see pages 139–40) and get a long piece of fabric, like a towel or a sheet, to be used as a sling.

2. Wrap the fabric around the cactus several times for good support, leaving at least a foot of loose material on each end to be used as carrying handles.

3. Gently tap the sides of the old pot to loosen the planting mix and plant from the container. Tip the cactus on its side and use the fabric sling to transport the cactus to the new location. (Two or more people make the process easier, especially for larger cacti—one can hold the pot, while the other holds the sling.)

4. (*a and b*) At its final destination, slide the pot off.

5. Place the root ball in the planting hole, and then pull the plant upright with the sling. Fill with the hole with more cactus mix, being careful not to cover up the cactus's crown above the root ball; this will help to avoid rot.

San Pedro cactus

(Echinopsis pachanoi)

If a frosty winter is in the cards and upright cacti are calling your name, the San Pedro cactus is your man. This cactus is likely the most foolproof to cultivate in the landscape, being cold-hardy down to the 20s F and not at all picky about growing conditions. Exponentially faster growing than many other columnar cacti, San Pedro adds a couple feet a year in favorable conditions. Its growth form is well branched, producing multiple trunks from the base, with secondary side arms emerging from the main trunks. Large colonies can develop in time, growing up to 15 feet

tall, but the cactus can be kept smaller with pruning. Its smooth skin is punctuated by tiny, white areoles with clusters of small spines, positioned evenly across its ribs and its color turns from bluish green to yellow in intense sun and drought.

Native to the Andes Mountains, San Pedro has naturalized throughout South America, where it is widely grown as an ornamental and medicinal plant. Also called *huachuma*, or cactus of the four winds, San Pedro (Saint Peter) is the center of a 4,000-year-old healing tradition that began with the pre-Columbian Chavín people of the northern Andean highlands.

Fantastic night-blooming flowers adorn the trunk at around five years of age. These oversized white trumpets seldom last more than a day, but their fragrance and ephemeral presence make a lasting impression. An effortless grower and beyond easy to propagate, San Pedro is a great cactus for the beginner.

PADDLE CACTI

The geometric library of cactus forms would not be complete without addressing the large genus *Opuntia*. Commonly called prickly pear because of the tiny spines that stud its pear-shaped fruits, its paddle-shaped leaves, *nopales* in Spanish, are staples in Mexican and Southwestern cuisine. Once peeled and despined, *nopales* are a versatile vegetable to use in salads and sautés, and to roast on the grill. In addition, the watermelon-like juice of the prickly pear fruit makes a refreshing tonic or a tasty alternative to the standard margarita—Opuntarita, anyone? For indigenous cultures of the southwestern United States and Mexico, this cactus has long been a staple food and source of medicine where little else grew. Even today, sap from the pads is used to treat wounds and reduce swelling, and the rich, red color of the fruit is used as a dye.

The genus *Opuntia* represents the dualistic nature of the plant kingdom: the plant's medicinal benefits are used to nurture health, but the cactus's sharp spines can inflict harm if it's approached carelessly. One brush against a prickly pear's body forges a lifelong memory. These cacti have two distinct types of spines: the barbed, hairlike bristles on the areoles, called glochids, and longer, sharper spines that can be lethal. Both types are present on most species, but some have only a network of glochids. These tiny, barbed prickles form in dense, hardly visible tufts around the areoles, and they are deceptively dangerous. In the bunny ears cactus (*Opuntia microdasys*), for example, white or yellow clusters of glochids look like fuzzy, touchable bumps, beguiling onlookers. Upon contact, however, hundreds of glochids detach from the pad, ruthlessly lodging in the skin, mouth, or coat. Their brittle composition and hooked tips make them notoriously difficult to remove.

Although you may think that such daunting armor would place prickly pear into a gardening no-fly zone, gardeners can safely work with them by donning an extra layer of protection. Wrap a towel around the cactus or wear heavy leather gloves to grip their spiny areas when working with them to avoid puncturing possibilities.

In contrast to the skyscraper heights of saguaro and San Pedro cacti, prickly pears have a wider, spreading profile with thick-jointed stems. What look like large, oblong-shaped leaves are actually flattened stem or pads, called cladodes. Each new cladode grows from the edge of a lower pad at a different angle, producing a striking assembly of planes reminiscent of an Alexander Calder mobile.

These beautiful cacti offer a strong reminder that some things in life are best appreciated at a distance. But they do boast an array of incredibly vibrant flowers, tasty fruits, and bulletproof qualities. In the landscape, their iconic forms create a signature Southwestern aesthetic, and they look stunning when surrounded by buffalo grass (*Bouteloua dactyloides*) and desert wildflowers.

Beavertail prickly pear

(*Opuntia basilaris*)

For pure flower power, the beavertail cactus (pictured above, left) is a tough, blooming groundcover form that sports a profusion of brilliant magenta flowers atop bluish paddles.

Spineless prickly pear

(*Opuntia cacanapa* 'Ellisiana')

This exceptionally smooth selection (pictured above, center) with clean, gray-green pads has no spines or glochids to deal with. It produces an abundance of yellow flowers that attract hummingbirds.

Santa Rita prickly pear

(*Opuntia santa-rita*, aka *O. violacea* var. *santa-rita*)

This purple prickly pear (pictured above, right) grows to a modest size—around 3 feet tall and 6 feet wide. Its best feature is its color-changing pads, whose colors vary according to surrounding temperatures. The almost round pads are turquoise-colored, with flushes of lavender and violet, with cold and heat stress. Any intensity in growth parameters seems to bring out more vibrant colors. Soft yellow flowers provide high contrast in the spring, especially when they're sited against a neutral backdrop of a stucco or adobe wall.

BARREL CACTI

Often romanticized as a bowl-shaped reservoir of water available for the stranded desert traveler, barrel cacti have much more to offer than a quick drink. Truth is, the alkaline, oxalate-laden water you might be able to squeeze out of a tight ball of spines would be further dehydrating, leaving you with a nasty bout of gastric distress to boot. It's best to approach these beauties with respect and let the legends fade into obscurity.

Barrel cacti comprise two main genera: *Echinocactus* species are commonly called golden barrels and originate from endangered populations in Mexico's Moctezuma River valley. *Ferocactus* species are spread throughout the Southwest— in California, Nevada, Arizona, and Texas.

Golden barrel cactus
(*Echinocactus grusonii*)

The golden barrel's mesmerizing arrays of yellow spines catch the light during the day, creating glowing globes, especially in late afternoon rays. Its tight, spherical profile is unique and provides contrast to other structural plants' trunks and large foliage in the landscape. Think of these cacti as whimsical garden adornments, an upgrade to decorative concrete or terracotta globes. Used in a minimalist fashion, golden barrels create a dramatic presence when paired with California fan palm (*Washingtonia filifera*), silvery beaked yucca (*Yucca rostrata*), and a variety of agaves to craft a living sculpture garden.

Each golden orb can reach 3 feet wide at maturity, forming many new pups from the base, in awe-inspiring asteroid-like colonies up to 6 feet wide. This hardy, long-lived species needs room for expansion, even though its growth seems slow initially. Because this cactus is self-sustaining when provided with good drainage and lots of sun, the only care required is seasonal weeding around its base. Specialty tweezers (see pages 151–52) work wonders for pulling oxalis from the base and between spiny ribs.

Fishhook barrel cactus

(Ferocactus wislizeni)

Also known as candy barrel or Arizona barrel cactus, the fishhook barrel cactus (pictured at left) is taller and more cold-hardy than the golden barrel. It is well distributed across the Mojave, Chihuahuan, and Sonoran deserts, and it also grows in and around Joshua Tree National Park as well as into Southern California and Mexico. Its habitat comprises dry, rocky slopes and washes, where competitors are few and triple-digit temperatures are frequent.

Young cacti are globe-shaped, but as decades roll on, they gradually elongate into pillar forms, reaching heights of 10 feet in granddaddy specimens.

Similar to their saguaro relatives, fishhook barrel cacti have a prominent ribbed structure that creates an accordion-like flexibility for water storage. The ribs are parallel throughout much of the plant's life but can take on a wavy character as they age and plants lean toward the sun. Take note of these curious details, which show exactly how beautiful an adaptation to nature's elements can be. While a stout cloak of spines may initially make these xerophytes seem unattractive, up close they are some of the cacti's most ornamental features. Often called fire barrels for their stout, bright red and fuchsia spines, their rich color is used to great effect in the landscape to echo warmer flower tones.

Celestial flowers appear in the crown in spring through fall. Pyramid-shaped buds open to a cup shape with dozens of delicate petals, resembling petite lotus flowers. Once the halo of blooms has closed, golden pineapple-shaped fruits develop as a grand finale. Known as cactus candy for their chewiness and sweet, lemony flavors, the fruits are often stewed to make jam or porridge.

With an increased public awareness of natural resource conservation, we need to give rigid succulents a chance in our water-wise gardens. The goal of this chapter is to show that you can achieve beauty in your garden using minimal water. By pushing past notions that edgier plants are too tricky to incorporate in our home landscapes, we can break our paradigm and ease in with an elegant Blue Glow agave in a tall container or an upright San Pedro cactus to spice up a boring wall. The following projects illustrate what can be accomplished in both small and large gardens with a trip to the spiny side.

OPPOSITE: Ball cactus (*Parodia magnifica*)

Sleek Lines and Spines

**A SAFARI SUNSET
CONEBUSH**
(*Leucadendron
'Safari Sunset'*)

B DRAGON TREE
(*Dracaena draco*)

C BLUE GLOW AGAVE
(*Agave* 'Blue Glow')

**D GOLDEN BARREL
CACTUS**
(*Echinocactus grusonii*)

E PARRY'S AGAVE
(*Agave parryi*)

The modern architecture aesthetic has long been complemented with gardens that include plants of strong form. Why not select species that play up the streamlined style of the home?

The smooth-textured stucco of this home is used to surface the retaining walls, creating a sense of continuity. The stepped walls and linear beds are perfect for showcasing a minimal selection of architectural plants. Including a limited number of plant species (five in this case) enables each plant grouping to stand out in the composition. Terraced retaining walls built from concrete, stone, or wood provide ideal backdrops for structural plants. But if you don't need or have retaining walls, you can use soil berms to provide a similar dynamic by juxtaposing plants at various elevations.

Add enough well-draining garden soil mix to fill the planters or build 12- to 24-inch berms if walls aren't desirable.

In the upper terrace or at the top of the berm, plant a row of Safari Sunset conebushes as a backdrop; spaced 3 to 4 feet apart. In front of the conebushes, plant a row of thick-trunked dragon trees, spaced 8 feet apart. Between the dragon trees, 3 feet apart, plant Blue Glow agaves, whose ruby-edged, dagger-shaped leaves will play off the red-saturated screen of conebushes.

In the lower terrace or lower area of the berm, plant more dragon trees to stagger the layout, creating a zig-zag effect. With their finer green foliage, dragon trees anchor the composition and offer a color bridge between the cool and hot colors of other plants.

Plant a group of golden barrel cacti and Parry's agaves between the dragon trees in the lower area. Use towels to wrap the barrel cacti before handling them (see page 99). Space both plants close together on 2-foot centers. As they mature, they will fill any gaps to provide a concentrated swath of the same species. (Although the landscape may feel underplanted at first, the simplicity of the layout will grow on you, or you can add more plants later if desired.)

Cover the entire planting area with $3/8$-inch gravel mulch.

Jurassic Hillside

A AFRICAN CANDELABRA
(*Euphorbia ammak*),
both variegated (such
as *E. ammak* 'Variegata')
and green selections

B SAN PEDRO CACTUS
(*Echinopsis pachanoi*)

C CHOLLA
(*Cylindropuntia* spp.)

D BLUE CANDLE
(*Myrtillocactus
geometrizans*)

E GOLDEN TORCH
(*Echinopsis spachiana*)

F PONYTAIL PALM
(*Beaucarnea recurvata*)

G PARRY'S AGAVE
(*Agave paryii*)

H PIG'S EARS
(*Cotyledon* spp.)

I AFRICAN MILK BARREL
(*Euphorbia horrida*)

J GOLDEN BARREL
CACTUS
(*Echinocactus grusonii*)

This hillside garden of epic proportions is one of the many masterpieces created by April Kluver and her late husband, Ryk, a legendary craftsman in Cayucos, California. When you're blessed with panoramic scenery, you can use plants of robust character to bridge the scale between the home and the expanse beyond. This is where buxom bottle palms, columnar cacti, and towering spurge come into play. On this scale, architectural plants work to frame the view instead of blocking it. But even if you lack a view, the dramatic plants in this garden illustrate how you can build your own stunning vista.

This garden is created by forming separate planting bed islands, surrounded by a sea of gravel. The winding gravel pathways provide garden access, and the islands enable select plants to be highlighted, with plenty of space in between. No matter the size of your garden, you can adjust the arrangement of island beds and paths to suit your space.

Amend the soil with 2 to 6 inches of well-finished compost (see pages 134–37). Surround each planting bed with a 6-inch wide border of 3 to 4 inches of chunky gravel.

Anchor several beds with upright African candelabras. You'll need to allow at least 12 feet between each to accommodate and showcase its impressive, spreading limbs. Wavy rows of small, black thorns line the margins of each trunk like stitching, accentuating the shapes of trunks and branches.

Around the African candelabras and in separate beds, add groupings of the supporting actors: San Pedro cacti, chollas, blue candles, golden torches, and ponytail palms. Use a single plant of each species in a bed, or plant each species in groupings of two to three.

Along the edges of the beds, plant groupings of low-growing Parry's agave, pig's ears, African milk barrel, and golden barrel cacti to light up the ground plane.

Mulch each planted bed with $^3/_8$-inch gravel, and fill the paths with $^3/_4$-inch gravel.

CHAPTER 6

Fusion Gardens

Succulent plants are strong front-runners in the water-wise gardening movement and add new and interesting dimensions to typical landscapes. New selections of agaves, aloes, and echeverias are being discovered, hybridized, and introduced to nurseries as fast as perennial penstemons. With a greater array of resource-friendly plants to choose from, gardeners are empowered to upgrade their landscapes to be both responsible and beautiful. An exciting generation of fusion-style gardening has emerged, blending traditional drought-tolerant plants with new succulents and xeric species, transporting the mixed garden to new heights.

In many public and private gardens, landscapers have incorporated succulents into their water-saving designs, rather than creating succulents-only spaces. The bold forms and colors of succulents blend well with the vibrant colors and textures of native perennials and grasses, desert wildflowers, and exotic proteas of South Africa, Australia, and the Mediterranean region.

Plant combinations are limited only by your imagination—in addition to your climate zone. Picture the varied texture of creeping hens and chicks (*Sempervivum* spp.) enlivening a filtered sun nook interplanted with coral bells (*Heuchera* spp.) and tree ferns; the chunky leaves of aloes, contrasting with the glossy foliage of mirror bush (*Coprosma* spp.), shaggy *Acacia cognata* 'Cousin Itt', and fuzzy lion's tail (*Leonotis leonurus*) blooms, underscored by the strappy foliage of *Cordyline* 'Cha-Cha', aeoniums, and *Echeveria* 'Afterglow' (pictured on page 30).

Local nurseries are bringing in richer palettes of durable, water-wise plants to support the growing demand, so encourage them to carry what you're looking for. If you do not live close to a nursery, you'll find a plethora of specialty nurseries online such as Silverhill Seeds in South Africa, Plant Delights Nursery in North Carolina, and Mountain Crest Gardens in California (see Resources, page 170, for more) that can facilitate the global exchange of unique plant material. Painting a mixed garden

Drought-tolerant grasses and blue-flowered germander sage (*Salvia chamaedryoides*) mix well with bromeliads and a variety of succulents in the author's fusion garden.

picture becomes increasingly dynamic once your canvas is expanded—from lacy trees and shrubs, to vibrant perennials, to structural grasses and reeds. Following are the main categories of companion plants I recommend to expand the succulent garden palette.

Small Trees

Trees provide vertical scale, structure, and drama to a garden layout. Creating relative scale and interest is best accomplished by using woody trees and shrubs that provide a greater statement, either in mass or girth or in architectural presence. Multiple-trunked trees, such as olives, acacias, madrones (*Arbutus* spp.), paperbarks (*Melaleuca* spp.), and palo verde (*Parkinsonia* spp.), can ground a vignette, screen an unsightly view, or frame an exceptional one. For a twist on the norm, look to a host of underused drought- and heat-tolerant trees from Texas, Mexico, and Arizona. Ironwood, Texas mountain laurel (*Sophora secundiflora*), feather bush (*Lysiloma watsonii*), desert willow (*Chilopsis* spp.), and chitalpa offer fine-textured foliage and open canopies in compact packages. These trees perform best in moderately warm climates away from the coastal fog belt. Trees in mixed plantings should be pruned annually to allow sunlight to penetrate through, giving adequate light to underplantings of shade-tolerant aeonium, cotyledon, and some echeveria.

Leucospermum 'Scarlet Ribbon'

Shrubs

Shrub parameters can get confusing in the horticultural lexicon, with some reaching tree size when mature and others remaining very compact throughout their lifetimes, such as dwarf conifers. Shrubs have historically played middle-child roles, living in the shadows of their taller tree siblings, unsure of where assert their personalities.

Tough native shrubs from North America, the Mediterranean region, and Down Under (Australia and New Zealand) boast compact habits, great blooming capacities, and elegant foliage. They offer improved options for gardeners across the board. You can finally let go of your power hedging tools!

The first group of plants ticking all the boxes of awesome shrubdom are members of the family Proteaceae (aka Protea). Hailing from South Africa, South America, and Australia, they carry an exotic presence in flower and form, plus a rugged constitution once established. Denizens of rocky, dry hillsides where wildfires frequently blaze, these plants have thick, corky bark to deter fire, and robust root systems that quickly regenerate new shoots after a burn. Proteas are equipped with specialized root systems that are engineered for extracting nutrients from poor soils.

Leucadendron 'Jester'

The Proteaceae family is named after the Greek god Proteus, who was known for his ability to change shape at will. Echoing this legend are species of *Grevillea*, *Leucadendron*, and *Leucospermum*, which are highly mutable (variable) across their combined 1,700 species. This family also spans tree forms towering to 150 feet (such as *Grevillea robusta*), down to demure 1-foot grevillea groundcovers (such as *G.* 'Australflora Fanfare'). What unites all members of the Proteaceae family are their distinctly cut foliage, adaptation to infertile soils, and supernatural flower forms. Ideal mates for the fusion garden, they need very little care and provide good anchors to work from.

What follows are descriptions of the three most landscape-friendly members of the family Proteaceae, suitable for the mixed garden, followed by the many-hued mirror bush (genus *Coprosma*) and several other water-wise shrubs. To move away from the heavy presence of traditionally used garden shrubs, I recommend species with ferny, divided, or needlelike leaves. Their light, airy textures blend well with the solid forms of succulents. Fine foliage is a strategic response to sunbaked conditions, as minimal leaf surface means less transpiration (water loss). Comparably, leaves with silver-gray, waxy surfaces or fuzzy surfaces also denote a plant's strategy to reflect intense sunlight and conserve moisture. Using these visual cues, we can choose plants that are not only visually enticing, but already inclined to drink responsibly in the garden.

Spider flower
(*Grevillea* spp.)

The genus *Grevillea* offers an array of species, from groundcovers, to shrubs, to large trees. Their foliage is quite variable between species, from needlelike, to ferny, to heavily margined like oak tree leaves, as demonstrated in the fabulous ground-hugging cultivar G. 'Austraflora Fanfare'. For a softer, woolly feel, look to G. *lanigera* 'Coastal Gem', G. *lavandulacea* 'Penola', and G. *lanigera* 'Prostrate'. These selections sport arching branches with dense sprays of grayish green leaves that are excellent weed-smothering groundcovers. From winter into spring, they erupt in dense clusters of pink and cream-colored flowers when not much else is blooming.

Medium-sized to large grevilleas provide midlayer or larger ballast, with large, dissected leaves with excellent textures. Even when plants are flowering, their unique foliage is a highlight for its year-round presence. Spider net grevillea (*G. fililoba*) is a come-and-pet-me selection, with threadlike foliage and a compact habit of 4 to 5 feet tall. Commanding more space in the 6 to 8 foot range are a few very floriferous cultivars worth growing, with stunning trusses of nectar-rich, bicolor flowers. *Grevillea* 'Peaches and Cream', 'Robyn Gordon', and 'Superb' (pictured opposite, left) all have attractive filigree leaves but differ in the color of their honey-laden flower clusters. The ferny foliage and intense colors of flowering grevilleas look stunning paired with chalky blue Parry's agave (*Agave parryi*), fan aloe (*Aloe plicatilis*), and red–flowering *Aloe* 'Blue Elf'.

Pincushions
(*Leucospermum* spp.)

Popularly known and grown as pincushions, these plants are delightful assets to the mild-climate garden. Best recognized by their extraterrestrial-inspired spring flowers, they are a major export in the florist trade, lasting up to a month in a vase. Compared to other proteas, they can be a bit fussy, demanding excellent drainage and sometimes dying for no clear reason. Pincushions are minimally frost-tolerant

and are best in temperatures above 30°F—or, even better, they can be moved into a greenhouse during the winter. Despite their idiosyncrasies, this plant's flowers are lust-worthy enough to keep visitors coming back for more.

Pincushions are less variable than other proteas, with most assuming evenly rounded forms. Most cultivars top out at around 4 to 6 feet tall and 6 to 8 feet wide at maturity. Their midsized stature is well used for stand-alone specimens or for backing a border. Foliage is leathery and thick, in shades of light green to gray, with fuzzy stems. The main flowering event bursts forth in late winter to spring, with a mature pincushion having hundreds of 4- to 8-inch flowers in full bloom over a period of months.

Flower colors range from orange and yellow, to burgundy and pink—sometimes on the same flower as it ages. A few notable selections are *L.* 'Tango', with long, slender foliage and an upright habit; *L.* 'Scarlet Ribbon', with large, salmon and crimson flower clusters; and the lower growing, golden nodding pincushion (*L.* 'Yellowbird'; pictured above, right), with gray leaves and canary-yellow flowers. For an exotic look, seek out stellar cultivar *L.* 'Brandi dela Cruz', a hybrid from the University of Hawaii with oversized glowing orange flowers. Kick off the spring festivities by pairing radiant pincushion blooms with the plum foliage of *Yucca* 'Blue Boy', *Yucca* Bright Star, and glowing coral aloe (*Aloe striata*).

Conebush

(*Leucadendron* spp.)

Conebushes are assets to the water-wise landscape, possessing a neatly structured habit of clean, colorful foliage. Native to the slopes of South Africa's Cape region, conebushes, like other members of the Protea family, possess a highly specialized morphology (form) in response to their unique native climate. What resemble the plant's brightly colored flowers are actually modified leaves, called bracts. As cold weather sets in, the saturation of the bract color morphs from red to burgundy or cream-colored to yellow, and then yellow to red again. Throughout the year, conebushes are chameleons, with foliage always in flux to keep things interesting.

Leucadendrons, probably the most popular landscaping proteas, can be used to create an extravagant niche in a garden border. A number of *L. salignum* cultivars, such 'Blush' (pictured above left), 'Summer Red', and 'Winter Red', have compact habits of 3 to 4 feet tall and are good midsized shrubs.

For a slightly larger profile in the 5 to 6 foot range, the sunshine conebush (*L.* 'Jester') offers a foliage jubilee, in hot-pink, burgundy, green, and cream colors in the same plant. Always a colorful joker, its foliage can be used to echo other warm tones in the landscape. The largest and widest used of the conebush clan, *L.* 'Safari Sunset', is an older hybrid that has earned its chops by thriving in clay soils and frosty temperatures down to the low 20s F. At 8 to 12 feet in maturity, it can be pruned annually to maintain a height of about 6 feet, if desired. Because conebushes possess vibrantly colored but small leaves, you can up the contrast by planting with them wide-leaved *Agave* 'Blue Flame' or smooth agave (*A. desmetiana*), or underplant with the rosy foliage of *Graptoveria* 'Fred Ives'.

Mirror bush
(*Coprosma* spp.)

Mirror bushes are variable plants from coastal areas and lowland forests in New Zealand, Hawaii, and other subtropical islands, where local breeders have recently produced many compelling new cultivars. Although some species are tree forms, much of the horticultural breeding efforts have focused on small, shrubby species of 3 to 5 feet, with variegated leaves in a rainbow of colors. In fact, because some cultivars' color display can lean toward gaudy and visually overwhelming, you're wise to consider their placement carefully in the garden. These shrubs are most showy in climates with mild winters and will do well with some shade in hot summer areas. Their dense foliage is the main affair, with tiny, polished, colorful leaves that appear to have been dipped in lacquer.

A few standout cultivars include *Coprosma* 'Fireburst' (pictured opposite, right), with pink and cream-colored foliage that intensifies to a fiery red in winter. The popular cultivar *C.* 'Tequila Sunrise' is the spiciest of the bunch, with yellow and lime-green leaves that morph into orange, or hot-pink in cooler weather. An underplanting of the yellow rainbow bush (*Portulacaria afra* 'Aurea'), with lemony leaves, adds even more tang. *Coprosma repens* 'Pink Splendor' is on the muted end, with a blend of pastel peach, pink, and cream-colored leaves that become even more alluring with a footing of lilac-pink *Echeveria* 'Perle von Nurnberg'.

Baja fairy duster
(*Calliandra californica*)

The Baja fairy duster is a densely branched, 4- to 5-foot shrub with fernlike, bipinnate foliage comprising tiny leaves divided into tinier leaflets. It's most notable for its flowers, with inconspicuous petals and long, bright red filaments that resemble pom-poms. Its smaller relative, at 1 to 3 feet, is the pink fairy duster (*C. eriophylla*), with translucent pink pom-poms that glisten in the sun.

Red bird of paradise and yellow bird of paradise

(Caesalpinia pulcherrima) and *(C. gilliesii)*

These South American species both resemble a tropical mimosa tree in a shrubby form, growing to 8 to 10 feet at maturity. Called the red bird of paradise *(Caesalpinia pulcherrima)* and yellow bird of paradise *(C. gilliesii;* pictured at left) their fiery flowers blaze through the entire summer in even the most intense heat. Although their lacy foliage suggests delicacy, these sister species are a staple of desert landscaping, being heat- and frost-tolerant. The largest difference between them is cold hardiness with *Caesalpinia pulcherrima* tolerating Zone 8 (lows of 10 to 20°F), while *C. gilliesii* can withstand the plummeting temperatures of Zone 5 (to –15°F) as shown in established specimens at the Denver Botanic Gardens.

Feathery cassia and silver leaf cassia

(Senna artemisioides) and *(S. phyllodinea)*

These leguminous (seedpod producing) characters feature threadlike (feather cassia; pictured below) and sickle-shaped (silver leaf cassia) foliage, in ghostly gray tones. Their heavy sprays of golden-yellow flowers display through the summer and fall and make a backdrop or screen in the garden. Both these shrubs are good solutions for problem areas—being wind-, heat-, and cold-tolerant to 20°F.

Flower Power

Humans have been mesmerized by flowers for as long as we've roamed the planet. What is it that beguiles us to stop and sniff, taking a moment to admire a flower's mysteries? A plant's highest energetic expression, the flower is a peak convergence of fragrance, symmetry, and spirit, designed to allure us all ever closer.

With an abundance of enticing flower colors available for water-wise landscapes, you can choose species of *Calylophus*, *Agastache*, *Penstemon*, and *Lobelia*—to name a few—to grace your garden. Many of these plants are commonly available through local nurseries, with more underused natives available by mail-order. (For information on nurseries, see the Resources section on page 169.) I highlight here only the most drought-tolerant perennials that thrive in a xeric landscape.

Berlandier's sundrops
(Calylophus berlandieri)

A shorty for the front of the border, the Berlandier's sundrop likes it warm and dry. Looking similar to a primrose with yellow, papery blooms, this sundrop blooms spring through fall, taking short breaks here and there to catch its breath. Threadlike foliage gives the 1-inch-tall mound a nice texture as it spreads to 3 feet wide. An adaptable plant that will bloom in full sun on the coast or in the interior, it tolerates reflected heat and can handle temperatures down to 0°F. Use this golden-flowered groundcover at the base of other plants, such as blue-leaved agaves, to create colorful harmony.

Hyssop

(Agastache spp.)

A few notable hyssops are denizens of Southwest desert zones and make great substitutes for thirsty garden perennials. In addition, this plant's edible flowers can be used as colorful and tasty additions to salads, and they are delicious brewed as tea. These members of the mint family have deliciously fragrant foliage and flowers in a rainbow of sunset hues. Licorice mint (*A. rupestris*), 2 to 3 feet tall, has an upright habit of willowy, silver foliage that smells unsurprisingly like licorice and root beer. Lavender calyxes hold hundreds of tubular orange, pink, and salmon-colored blooms from summer to fall, forming a sunset-colored soiree. Other rugged, hardy hyssops such as Texas hummingbird mint (*A. cana*), orange hummingbird mint (*A. aurantiaca*), and and *A.* 'Purple Haze' (pictured at left) light up the dry, Zone 5 (to –15°F) garden. Their wispy statures also look at home popping up between rosettes of agaves, spiky yuccas, prickly pears, and barrel cacti. Because they thrive in low-nutrient soils with little water, tough love is best for hyssops; they can easily rot with overwatering.

Beardtongue

(Penstemon spp.)

Natural favorites for the garden border, modern hybrid penstemons are showy, but they aren't drought-tolerant, unlike the majority of native species. The natives are also where it's at for beauty and sound character. You can spot a tough beardtongue by its foliage either being very slender, such as the pineleaf beardtongue (*P. pinifolius*; pictured opposite, on left) or having a glaucous coating (such as the hackberry beardtongue, *P. subulatus*). The desert beardtongue (*P. pseudospectabilis*) has many nicknames, including canyon penstemon and rosy desert beardtongue (for its rosy red, foxglove-like flowers). It grows in desert washes, among my favorite succulent plant partners: boulders, ocotillo (*Fouquieria splendens*), and Joshua trees (*Yucca brevifolia*). The showy penstemon, *P. spectabilis*, has crystalline violet and pink blooms that

hummingbirds can't get enough of! These plants are heat lovers, hardy to a searing 115°F and near 0°F in the cold months. They need well-drained, lean soil, and can be left alone for the most part. Add a little water to help them get established, but then keep the hose coiled.

Mexican lobelia
(Lobelia laxiflora)

Most folks think of lobelia as a shade-loving trailing plant used in hanging baskets and annual arrangements, but this plant is so much more! While some tender, blue-flowered species are from South Africa, their hardier cousin is native to the dry climates of Mexico and Central and South America. Mexican lobelia (pictured above, right) looks similar to a densely leaved beardtongue, with slender, medium-green foliage that forms a clump about 2 to 3 feet tall, and bright red, tubular flowers with yellow throats. It blooms brilliantly from spring until fall in mild climates and a slightly shorter period in hotter areas.

Cold-hardy to 0° F, this drought-tolerant plant gets no water in my coastal garden, except for winter rainfall, where it nests happily among the century plant *Agave chazaroi*, lipstick echeveria (*Echeveria agavoides*), and Bullock's bottle brush (*Aloe taurii*). It needs pruning once or twice a year to remove spent blooms—and that's about it. Beautiful year-round, it's one of the showiest water-wise perennials available.

QUICK-REFERENCE GUIDE TO COMPANION PLANTS FOR SUCCULENTS

TREES	SHRUBS TO SMALL TREES	PERENNIALS
Most olives (*Olea* spp.), pruned to an open form to let light through to underplantings	Most Proteacea: Grevillea, leucadendron, leucospermum, banksia, protea	Hyssops: Texas hummingbird mint (*Agastache cana*) Orange hummingbird mint (*A. aurantiaca*) Licorice mint (*A. rupestris*)
Acacias: River wattle (*Acacia cognata*) Knifeleaf acacia (*A. cultriformis*) Shoestring acacia (*A. stenophylla*)	Fairy dusters: Baja fairy duster (*Calliandra californica*) Pink fairy duster (*C. eriophylla*)	Sundrops: Berlandier's sundrop (*Calylophus berlandieri*)
Strawberry trees: *Arbutus* 'Marina' *A. unedo*	Yellow bird of paradise (*Caesalpinia gilliesii*) Red bird of paradise (*C. pulcherrima*)	Beardtongues: Desert beardtongue (*Penstemon pseudospectabilis*) Showy penstemon (*P. spectabilis*) Pineleaf beardtongue (*P. pinifolius*)
Paperbarks: Broad-leaved paperbark (*Melaleuca quinquenervia*) Pink melaleuca (*M. nesophila*)	Shrubby cassias: Feathery cassia (*Senna artemisioides*) Silver leaf cassia (*S. phyllodinea*)	Lobelias: Mexican lobelia (*Lobelia laxiflora*) Devil's tobacco (*L. tupa*)

TREES	SHRUBS TO SMALL TREES	PERENNIALS
Palo verdes: Mexican palo verde (*Parkinsonia aculeata*) Blue palo verde (*P. florida*)	Ocotillo (*Fouquieria splendens*)	Most sages: Germander sage (*Salvia chamaedryoides*) Cleveland sage (*S. clevelandii*) Baby sage (*S. microphylla*)
Texas mountain laurel (*Sophora secudiflora*)	Water willows: Chuparosa (*Justicia californica*) Mexican honeysuckle (*J. spicigera*)	Most spurges: Mediterranean spurge (*Euphorbia characias*) cultivars Gopher spurge (*E. rigida*) Fire sticks (*E. tirucalli* 'Sticks on Fire')
Chitalpas: ×*Chitalpa tashkentensis* 'Pink Dawn' ×*Chitalpa tashkentensis* 'Morning Cloud'	Feather bush (*Lysiloma watsonii*)	Milkweeds: narrow-leaved milkweed (*Asclepias fascicularis*) showy milkweed (*A. speciosa*)
Desert willow (*Chilopsis linearis*)	Jerusalem sage (*Phlomis russeliana*)	Snapdragons: Island snapdragon (*Galvezia speciosa*) Baja snapdragon (*Galvezia juncea*)
Desert ironwood (*Olneya tesota*)	Pearl bluebush (*Maireana sedifolia*)	Majorcan teucrium (*Teucrium cossonii*)

Putting It All Together

My goal is to suggest new and intriguing selections for a beautifully mixed garden. I wrote this book in hopes of spurring a garden transition—from a typical, water-thirsty, perennial-filled garden, into a composition with greater variety, depth, and style, that requires less (or no) water. You can plan your garden vignettes as you would decorate for a party. Develop a theme, and then invite the guests that will bring your plans to fruition. It may be a south-of-the-border fiesta, with colorful plants from Texas, California, and Mexico that can turn up the heat. Or it could be a sizzling desert oasis theme, with blue palo verde (*Parkinsonia florida*) for an airy green canopy, spineless prickly pear (*Opuntia ellisiana*) for bulky leaves and striking form, *Hesperaloe* species for spiky textures and tall blooms, and Hartweg's sundrops (*Calylophus hartwegii*) and Mexican lobelia (*Lobelia laxiflora*) for fronting the border with splashes of yellows and reds.

The following projects show you how to create your own garden festivities.

Welcome Home

A BEAR'S BREECH
(*Acanthus mollis*)

B MOUNTAIN ASTELIA
(*Astelia nervosa*)

C RAY OF LIGHT CENTURY PLANT
(*Agave attenuata* 'Ray of Light')

D GYPSUM CENTURY PLANT
(*Agave gypsophila*)

E ISLAND MANZANITA
(*Arctostaphylos insularis* 'Canyon Sparkles')

F CANYON PRINCE WILD RYE
(*Leymus condensatus* 'Canyon Prince')

G SAN MIGUEL ISLAND BUCKWHEAT
(*Eriogonum grande* var. *rubescens*)

H ANCHOR BAY CEANOTHUS
(*Ceanothus gloriosus* 'Anchor Bay')

Like a hug from an old friend, a home's entry garden should offer comfort, with a design that confirms that all is well with the world. This arrangement of plants is the first thing you see when you arrive at my home garden. A northern exposure provides low light levels, so the focus here is on year-round foliage interest instead of flowers. The bold leaves of dark green bear's breech (*Acanthus mollis*) and the variegated century plant *Agave attenuata* 'Ray of Light' are positioned to provide a good foil for the fine-textured grasses and red-flowered San Miguel Island buckwheat (*Eriogonum grande* var. *rubescens*). A chunk of local driftwood and a rusty bollard light anchor the composition and speak to its coastal environs.

Amend the soil with 2 to 6 inches of well-finished compost (see pages 134–37).

Place a piece of large driftwood and a bollard light (or boulder, pottery, or a sculpture) as main focal points to signal the home's entry and ground the arrangement. (In my garden, the two features are placed adjacent to one another, with the pale bark of the driftwood highlighted when the bollard lights up after dark.)

Plant coarse-leaved bear's breech behind the bollard, a single clumping mountain astelia next to the bollard, and two or three century plants surrounding the driftwood to form a backdrop for the finer textured species in the foreground.

In the midground area, plant several island manzanita shrubs and wild rye grass to provide verticality and texture.

Plant the foreground with San Miguel Island buckwheat and creeping Anchor Bay ceanothus to colonize the low area and provide clouds of color in spring and summer.

Top dress the garden with 2 or 3 inches of black mulch to provide additional contrast to the vibrant foliage.

Restful Retreat

A PINK MELALEUCA
(*Melaleuca nesophila*)

B SLIM BOTTLEBRUSH
(*Callistemon viminalis* 'Slim')

**C MARINA STRAWBERRY
TREE**
(*Arbutus* 'Marina')

**D BLUE FLAME
CENTURY PLANT**
(*Agave* 'Blue Flame')

**E FIREBURST MIRROR
PLANT**
(*Coprosma* 'Fireburst')

**F PROSTRATE WOOLLY
GREVILLEA**
(*Grevillea lanigera*
'Prostrate')

**G RAY OF LIGHT
CENTURY PLANT**
(*Agave attenuata*
'Ray of Light')

H GIANT RED AEONIUM
(*Aeonium* 'Cyclops')

This eclectic design draws from a palette of Mediterranean, Californian, and Australian plants, demonstrating a seamless integration of water-wise species. Layers of varied screening are built up with pink melaleuca, strawberry tree, and bottlebrush to add depth and create a buffer from the active neighborhood corner. Smaller scale garden trees like the strawberry tree are best pruned with an open trunk and canopy to make room for a planting layer underneath.

Groups of bold-leaved agaves hold down the midground area, along with softly spreading mirror plants and woolly grevillea. The broken shade under the strawberry tree creates the perfect environment for aeoniums and variegated agaves that prefer relief from full sun. A small swath of lawn leading to the seating area provides an interior respite and a buffer between house and garden. Here, succulents blend well with other water-wise plants to bring a lush variety of shapes, colors, densities, and textures in the garden.

If you have an exposed lot and desire more privacy, this garden design provides a template for creating a buffer between the house and public areas through layers of trees, shrubs, and succulents.

Amend the soil with 2 to 6 inches of well-finished compost (see pages 134–37). Mark out a small, asymmetrical lawn space surrounded by planting beds.

Plant several pink melaleucas and bottlebrushes to buffer the property borders between the garden and the street.

Establish a focal point and vertical interest by planting a multitrunked strawberry tree at a central position in the garden. Its sculptural, cinnamon-colored trunk and large leaves anchor the mixed plantings surrounding it.

Plant one or more pink melaleucas at the base of the strawberry tree to establish continuity and mark the transition between the ornamental plantings and the lawn.

To develop plant layering in the foreground, start with planting 2 to 5 Blue Flame century plants to provide eye-catching movement. Place a coral-colored mirror plant across from the century plants, next to the strawberry tree. Next to the mirror plant, place a ground-hugging woolly grevillea.

A bit behind the strawberry tree, between the tree and the street, add 3 to 5 soft-leaved, shade-tolerant Ray of Light century plants, plus 3 giant red aeoniums for contrast.

Spread 2 or 3 inches of fir bark mulch over the planting area, then lay down a swath of sod for the lawn.

Agave 'Blue Flame'

CHAPTER 7

Tools, Techniques, and Plant Care

Of course, there can be no garden without a gardener. The landscape is a living environment that provides an opportunity for a caretaker to build an insightful relationship with the plants that grow there. This relationship with your garden is interactive and essential to its well-being, and to yours. As with any type of husbandry, gardening involves give and take, sickness and health, and some sacrifice and learning along the way. A garden is an ongoing labor of love, and you can always spot a garden in balance with its keeper—it projects a certain radiance throughout the seasons.

Every gardener needs the right tools and techniques to maintain a healthy garden. This chapter provides practical nuts-and-bolts information that builds on the previous chapters about plant specifics. We'll dig into the physical components of soil amending, watering, planting, dealing with pests, choosing useful tools, and understanding what plants need. Earlier chapters presented the *what* and the *why*; this chapter offers the *how* to care for your personal Shangri-La.

If you're new to playing in the plant kingdom, these straightforward techniques will explain how to integrate plants soundly into the environment, and how to care for them after they are in the ground. Starting off, keep in mind that although this book is about creating a stunning, low-maintenance landscape, this is different from a *no-maintenance* approach. It's true that many of these plants can take care of themselves, more or less, once established, but we are cultivating a landscape because we want it to look, well, cultivated and cared for.

Think of your garden as more than a collection of plants. Think of it as an ecosystem brimming with life at every juncture. When you notice issues such as insect damage, gopher holes, yellowing leaves, or other certain signs of stress, they are simpler to manage if you take care of them quickly. I recommend that you make a habit of strolling through your garden regularly to check in with your plants,

Artfully symmetrical rosettes of *Agave* 'Kissho Kan' in the foreground and *Agave victoriae-reginae* in the center, back.

making time to enjoy their highlights and seasonal shifts, and evaluating potential issues. Think of it as a soulful stroll, where you can slow down and tune in to the rhythms of nature and your cocreated garden. Try cruising the loop in bare feet for the most grounding experience.

The Real Dirt (Soil)

Why is healthy soil so prized, while dirt is despised, when they actually seem like one and the same? Although these colloquial terms are often used interchangeably, they refer to two entirely different things.

In short, dirt is basically dead soil, void of the organic matter, microorganisms, earthworms, and nutrients that make soil alive. Dirt happens after we remove or use up all life from the soil or lay impermeable materials (such as asphalt) on top, suffocating any vitality below. Soil, on the other hand, is a living, dynamic matrix comprising a prime ratio of water, nutrients, minerals, oxygen, and magnetic forces that create an ecosystem for plants to thrive. The synergy with which these mostly invisible ingredients work together in an underground collective shapes the visible architecture of our landscape. The more alive the underground soil flora, the more vigorous the health of our plants and the ecosystem as a whole. As below, so above.

When you're starting out with a new plot, it's helpful to know what type of soil you have to work with. Dig down about 18 inches in your garden soil and collect a sample there. You can purchase an affordable $20 to $30 soil test kit from a local soil lab or cooperative extension to analyze your soil sample, which includes a complete battery of what's in your terra firma. It will spell out the critical parameters such as pH (the amount of alkalinity or acidity), nutrient levels, and relative ratios of organic matter, sand, silt, and clay. Knowing these parameters will tell you how best to amend your soils, usually with compost. Often, soil test reports include their own recommendations based on findings.

Without using a proper soil test, you can use a "look-and-feel" assessment to identify your native type of soil. If your soil feels fine and grainy in your hand, it has a high sand content. Sand is low in nutrients and has a loose structure that enables water to pass through it readily—quickly leaching nutrients. You can amend sandy soil with 3 to 6 inches of compost to increase its water-holding capacity and supply organic nutrients. Also, if a shovel easily penetrates into the soil, you probably have sandy soil.

Clay soils, on the other hand, are tightly structured and form heavy clods that are difficult to dig into. The large surface area of clay particles are well equipped to hold onto water, and vitamins and minerals. Clay is easily compacted, so getting oxygen and water to permeate clay's dense construction is the first order of business to unlock its potential. Compost will readily improve clay-based soils; its microbial richness and humus content open up the structure of clay particles, as millions of bacteria go to work every day to make the soil more workable and easier for roots to proliferate. Clay soils need less compost than sandy soils: 2 to 4 inches of compost is a good place to start.

Fear not if your haven-to-be resembles an old dirt road. Living compost is pure magic for restoring even the most wronged patches of earth back to their former glory. Compost is simply an aggregation of decomposed organic materials. It's teeming with a variety of nutrients, microbes, fungi, and other life forms that build up the soil food web, the community of organisms living all or part of their lives in the soil. In nature, twigs, branches, leaves, and cones will eventually decompose on their own to form mounds of biologically rich material. With compost, we are trying to replicate nature's process of building soil, but in a shorter time frame, by amending poor soils with a microbe-rich and full-spectrum soil supplement.

Compost also acts as a sponge, holding nutrients and water until they are requested by actively mining roots. While chemical fertilizer provides only a short list of specific plant nutrients, compost provides a broader spectrum of food for the entire soil matrix. You can use compost in conjunction with slow-release, organic fertilizer for a targeted effect, but it's best to steer clear of chemical-laden bags of N-P-K–labeled fertilizers that are heavy in salts, which can end up as chemical runoff. Excess salt also acidifies soils, damaging the microbial balance and structure of soil in the long run.

As organic matter decomposes, you will notice compost lets off puffs of steam as you work with it, indicating its vitality. Not all compost is created equally, however, so look for a product that is dark in color, that smells like the forest, and that has a fine, crumbly texture. If the compost smells of ammonia or another off-putting aroma (like rotting matter), it's not finished compost. Don't accept compost that includes large chunks of bark or other coarse organic material, because these materials require further decomposition. You can purchase compost in bags or bulk or make it at home using a variety of techniques. Bagged compost can be convenient for small potting projects, but much of its microbial vitality may have been lost if it was pasteurized or smothered in the package for too long. Bulk compost from a landscape supply yard is usually best, at a fraction of the cost of bagged products, and it can be delivered right to your front yard.

If this were a book on vegetable gardening, I would recommend using as much rich compost as possible, but since we are working with plants that are already adapted to lean soils, we can be light-handed in adding nutrients. In residential conditions, many soils are disturbed, eroded, and compacted by construction and machinery, which may have occurred years prior to our arrival. If you are fortunate enough to have rich soil with its topsoil intact, you probably won't need to amend it. But this isn't the reality for most of us; improving the quality of our garden soil is essential for success on any level of cultivation, including gardening with succulents. Across the board, plants that are given a head start with healthy soil conditions overcome transplant shock more quickly and adapt readily to new conditions.

Compost is food, and not just fertilizer, and the nutrients it contains feed and stabilize plants as they establish. Newly planted, nutrient-hungry plants such as perennials and grasses digest most of the healthy ingredients in compost in about two years; at that point, compost needs to be reapplied to keep growth vigorous.

Succulent plants, on the other hand, digest nutrients in a more gradual way: They respond kindly to healthy soil conditions at planting when they receive an initial nutrient boost, but by the time a succulent has established itself in a few years, the soil nutrients have been reduced, which suits it in the long run. You can top dress with compost every few years if you want plants to grow stronger, but it's usually unnecessary to do this, because succulents are programmed for slow and steady growth in poor soils.

Adding compost to the soil before installing these rugged plants may seem unnecessary, and some schools of thought support planting in unamended soil. In my experience, however, although this barebones approach can work, it can also result in stunted growth and a lower percentage of survivors. With proper soil preparation, your plants gain momentum right out of the gate, and survival rates in the 90th percentile are a reality.

Calculating Your Soil, Compost, Mulch, and Stone Needs

The team at a local landscape supply center can be helpful in determining material needs in addition to these general guidelines. Landscape materials are measured either in yards or tons, depending on their density. Loose materials such as soil, compost, mulch, and gravel are measured by the yard at landscape suppliers and some nurseries, and they are measured by the cubic foot in bags sold at many nurseries and garden centers. Bags of mulch and amendments often contain 1.5 to 3 cubic feet of material. If you purchase bags, use this conversion to estimate how much you'll need: 27 cubic feet = 1 cubic yard.

Buying bulk materials by the yard is less expensive overall, and most supply houses will deliver materials, or you can haul them yourself. One yard of loose material such as mulch, gravel, or soil will cover a 150-square-foot area at 2 inches thick—a common depth for mulches, gravels, and soils. So, if you have 600 square feet to cover with 2 inches of mulch, you'll need 4 yards of material (600 ÷ 150 = 4). If you want to amend at a 4 or 6 inches in depth, simply double or triple your calculated amount for a 2-inch depth. In this case, a 4-inch depth will require 8 yards, and a 6-inch depth will require 12 yards of material.

For adding deeper amendments, stacking cobble (rocks that are smaller than boulders and larger than gravel), or adding boulders, use a volume calculation: multiply length × width × depth to determine cubic footage. Suppose, for example, that you'd like to form a natural rock border out of stone cobbles that is 1 foot tall, 1 foot wide, and 20 feet long. Your rock volume needed is 20 cubic feet. (20 ft. × 1 ft. × 1 ft.). Cobble is sold by the yard or by weight, depending on size, so I will calculate both methods to cover all the bases. To convert to yards, use the equation 27 cubic feet = 1 yard. Divide 27 by 20 to see that you need 1.35 yards of cobble. To convert yards to tons, multiply by 1.3 (1.35 yards × 1.3 = 1.755 tons). To finally get to pounds, multiply your tonnage by 2000. So 1.75 tons × 2000 = 3510 pounds.

FORMULAS:

1 yard = 27 cubic feet (L × W × D)

1 yard = 150 square feet material coverage (L × W) at 2-inch depth

Yards of material × 1.3 = tons of material

Tons of material × 2000 = total pounds (2000 pounds per ton)

Bermology: Get Elevated

Most succulents and related plants hail from areas with well-draining (often sandy or rocky) soil. Don't underestimate the importance of good drainage as a vital component in a healthy garden. Nutrients and pH (the amount of alkalinity or acidity) in the soil can be right on, but if soggy, anerobic (low oxygen) areas persist in your garden, drought-tolerant plants will be difficult to grow.

Positive drainage results from having porous soils, where water can easily move through the substrate, allowing oxygen and aerobic (high oxygen) microbes to fill pore spaces. The drainage process is also enhanced by the pitched grades of the native lands of many succulent plants. Sloped terrain greatly increases drainage capacity, with a little help from gravity. If you aren't blessed with sloped terrain or sandy soil, you can improve your soil's drainage capacity in a couple of ways. The most straightforward method is to create topography by mounding soil into berms.

Building berms of amended soil is the secret weapon to growing choice plants in poorly draining, native soil. Contouring soil into raised berms of 4 to 18 inches tall enables the crowns of the plants to be planted into more accommodating and faster draining soil. The crown, the area where the above-ground stem or trunk meets the roots as they fan out into the soil, is the plant's Achilles heel. If this critical area stays wet for too long, it can easily rot, and with rot, succulents will quickly suffer. As long as the soil around the crown drains well, the deeper roots can adapt in time to the heavier soils below.

In addition to providing better drainage, sculpted berms can be used to create rolling areas of interest in the garden, mimicking a natural landscape. Nature organizes her beauty into curvilinear and organically shaped forms, so why not echo rising and falling elevations on our home turf? Raised mounds of soil make excellent spots for sinking a few boulders to create rock outcroppings, which in turn create planting pockets in which succulents can naturalize. Line low areas below berms with stone cobbles to shuttle out drainage water, or populate this area with plants that appreciate more moisture.

Dry wells, drainage inlets, and a series of gravel-lined French drains are other possible solutions to water woes. These constructed drainage systems slow down the momentum of water with layers of rock, allowing water to percolate deeper into the soil profile. Piped drainage requires laborious trenching and underground work, but it can be effective at moving water from stagnant areas to other zones, where it can be used by deeper diving plant roots. Instead of shuttling valuable rainwater to the

Agave 'Blue Glow' (left foreground), *Agave* 'Blue Flame' (center), and dune aloe (*Aloe thraskii*; right) thrive on this constructed berm.

curb, use gravel-lined French drains to send water deep into the soil profile for your plants to draw from as the upper layers of soil dry in hot, dry climates. Encouraging plants roots to go deep, searching for water, is how true drought tolerance in garden conditions is developed.

Planting Prowess

Compost offers the greatest benefit when it's mixed into the top 2 to 4 inches of soil, where most feeder roots grow. No matter the layout of the planting area, blanketing the entire surface in at least 2 to 4 inches of compost is the most effective way to encourage this distribution. As you install plants, you can mix the compost into the soil around them. Surrounded by a good compost mix, roots are encouraged to radiate outward, seeking nutrients beyond the planting hole. (If you already have established plants that need a full-spectrum boost, pull back the mulch and top dress them with 1 or 2 inches of compost. Then reapply the mulch.)

Beyond amending the soil with compost, you can achieve planting success by following these best practices:

1. Dig a hole about twice as wide as the pot. If the existing soil is dry, fill the planting hole with water and let it saturate, so that the plant will start with its roots in a moist environment. Dry soil can wick water away from the root ball and stress the plant.

2. To loosen the plant from the pot, tap the sides of the pot firmly but gently.

3. Then carefully flip the pot upside down and, while holding the crown between your fingers, ease out the plant.

4. If gophers are present, always protect plants by placing them in a wire basket before placing in the planting hole—more on these baskets on page 149. Place the plant into the planting hole, making sure the crown of the plant is level with or 1 inch above the existing grade. It's better to err toward planting on the high side since loose soil will settle over time. Planting too low results in the crown resting in a depression, where it may stay wet, causing the dreaded root and crown rots.

5. Backfill the planting hole with loosened native soil, mixing compost into the top 3 inches where the feeder roots are concentrated.

6. Press to firm the soil around the root ball with your hands.

7. Using some of the soil you removed while creating the hole, form a 2-inch tall full-circle well or ridge around the plant, 6 inches away from the plant. (You'll read more about this on page 143.) If you're planting on a slope, create a horseshoe-shaped well on the low side of the plant to capture surface run off from the slope above. These wells help capture and hold water where new roots can access it. The planting well will naturally erode over the first year as plants get established.

8. Water around the plant thoroughly to settle and moisten the soil. Mulch around the plant with gravel, woodchips, or other organic materials. Gravel is best for plants that prefer quickly draining soil such as cacti, euphorbias, and other desert species that don't appreciate any residual water near the crown. Aloes, agaves, crassulas, and many other succulents can be mulched with woodchips (which retain more water) for a softer look.

Water Wisdom

Watering plants is an art that take some practice to understand and master. Some gardeners misunderstand the watering needs of succulent plants. Despite their intelligent ability to store hydration onboard, succulents do appreciate occasional water, and they need it to survive.

The most critical factor with watering revolves around timing and saturation. A deep and infrequent watering schedule is most applicable to drought-tolerant plants, rather than frequent, light sprinklings. Brief applications enable water to penetrate into the upper soil layers only, encouraging only the growth of surface roots that dry out easily in warmer conditions. Deeper soaks can penetrate down 12 to 36 inches or more, encouraging deeper roots and greater drought tolerance.

Succulents are built to withstand long periods between hydration, and it's best to allow the soil to dry out before you apply more water. If the soil is regularly irrigated every few days, its stays waterlogged, and oxygen doesn't have a chance to diffuse through the soil; this can result in rotting plant roots and crowns. Weaning yourself from overwatering can take some unlearning if you are accustomed to watering regimens for typical thirsty perennials, which can be irrigated multiple times a week. I think that most landscapes are chronically overwatered, which

pushes excessive growth, leading to unnecessary maintenance, early plant death, and wasted resources. When you're gardening with drought-tolerant succulents, adjust irrigation schedules to water less frequently as plants become established. If you continue frequent watering throughout a plant's life, you're not leveraging the water-saving abilities of these species. Why plant drought-tolerant plants and then water and feed them like petunias? As succulent gardeners, our mantra should be this: the faster plants grow, the quicker they die. If we can understand the advantages of gardening for long life over instant gratification, nature will have imbued one of her greatest lessons.

When plants are pushed with excess water (and fertilizer), unbalanced growth results. Uneven, waterlogged growth can cause plants to grow leggy and actually collapse under their own weight. Excessive growth is also very appealing to aphids and mealybug pests looking for a sugary snack.

Establishing a garden should include a stepped plan for automatic irrigation or hand-watering, where water application is decreased as plants become established and more self-sufficient. A general timeline for watering goes like this:

- The first year, succulents require regular soil moisture as they establish root systems. Depending on your amended soil's ability to hold moisture and the warmth of your climate, you can water plants once or twice a week.

- In their second year, plants are becoming established and need only weekly watering.

- As year three rolls around, you can water once every few weeks to every few months.

- At year four, apply water only as needed, with some species not requiring any supplemental moisture at all, other than rainfall.

Keep in mind that this is a general prescription, with warmer and harsher areas requiring more frequent water to establish plants, so adjust to your climate as plants indicate.

The ideal time to water is in the early morning, when evaporation is minimal and plants can take in a full drink to prepare for the day's sun and warmth. To achieve the best soil saturation, you should have created a soil well around the plant when you installed it (refer to step 7 of the agave planting, page 140). The well acts as a basin around the plant, directing water to the root area instead of allowing it to run off.

If hand-watering, fill the well with water three times, letting it drain between fills to accomplish good saturation. Alternate the timing of well draining by filling up the wells of nearby plants to keep the process moving. If the soil is dry or heavy, it may take a bit of time for each well to drain fully.

If using a drip systems, install emitters that disperse $1/2$ gallon per hour to 1 gallon per hour to give an adequate volume of water, and let the system run for 30 minutes. (Large volume emitters such as 2 to 4 gallon per hour produce water faster than the soil can absorb—creating run-off.)

After watering, check that the soil is saturated by extending your index finger 3 inches into the soil around the plant to sense moisture. If the water in a well hasn't penetrated that deeply, add more water until deeper saturation is reached.

A Watering Case Study

My demonstration garden—a mild, fog-dappled, USDA Zone 10a garden in Morro Bay, California—is eight years old. Coastal California is considered a Mediterranean climate, with dry summers and winter rainfall and no measurable moisture occurring from late spring to fall. The garden was watered once a week for the first two years, and then restricted to the following schedule: In dry-winter years, I limited drip irrigation of proteas and succulent plants to once a quarter for two or three hours, providing a deep soak. In wet winters with more than 20 inches of rainfall, I tested the plants' tolerance, providing no supplemental water throughout the year, and all species sailed right through. From experiments in my own and other's landscapes, I have found that in coastal and warmer landscapes, succulents and Mediterranean plants need less water, are more stress-tolerant, and do not require regular hand-watering or automatic irrigation once established.

Do not water again until succulents develop subtle wrinkles in their leaves and droop slightly; this indicates that their internal water pressure has dropped (because the plants have depleted much of their water reserves). It's important to be able to diagnose whether your plants are receiving too much or too little water:

- When overwatered, succulent leaves look mushy and fall off the plant when touched.

- When underwatered, plant leaves will droop and wrinkle, losing their plumpness.

It's easier to revive an underwatered plant than an overwatered one, so it's best to take the watering approach of less is more. If you are gardening in an area with high rainfall and don't need to add supplemental water, try planting succulents in soil berms to encourage water to flow away from their crowns.

Plant colors arising from summer stress can be attractive in aloes, and many Crassula family species (*Sedum*, *Echeveria*, *Kalanchoe*), whose leaves turn deeper shades of red as a stress response to intense sunlight and little water. Enjoy the kaleidoscopic foliage show as a good sign that you're not overwatering. The best colors and forms develop in plants that have to earn their keep! Even when stressed, established plants return to grace as the rains come in the fall.

Shaking Off the Chill

To create a low-maintenance and long-lived landscape plan, you should ensure that most plants in your garden are well adapted to your USDA hardiness zone. Growing a few unique species that are on the margins of your hardiness zone, however, is worth the effort if you don't mind taking extra measures during cold weather. In addition, early or late in the season when frost can nip tender new growth, a little temperature buffer from the elements can help the plants survive.

Frost cloth offers a good insulation solution and can increase the air temperature surrounding plants by 3° to 6°F, depending on its thickness. This might not seem like much, but when temperatures plummet, each degree earned under the cloth can help prevent plants from freezing. Covering plants with blankets and sheets is less effective, because these coverings block the sun's rays; the sun is actually the key element that enables heat to build during the daytime. Permeable frost cloth enables the sun's accumulated warmth to be maintained into the colder night hours. Frost

Chalk dudleya
(*Dudleya*
pulverulenta)

cloth also breathes, so it won't overheat like plastic, so there's no need to remove it during the daytime.

To keep the cloth off delicate plants, use lightweight stakes to prop up the material a few inches above the plant for a tenting effect, which also maintains an insulating air layer. Attach the edges of the cloth to the ground and secure with stakes or bricks to complete the microclimate.

Frost cloth is available online in various roll sizes, and you can also purchase preformed frost jackets for larger plants, as well as drawstring bags to protect hanging plants. Covering plants shouldn't need to be a regular part of your winter regimen, but frost covers can go a long way toward getting a new or favorite plant established.

Plant Predators

All insects have a purpose, although it's hard to recognize a pest's value after it's mutilated a precious plant in an overnight feast. Most garden pests appear cyclically, emerging in waves at certain times of year when peak opportunities are present.

Piercing and sucking insects such as aphids and mealybugs often appear in spring, when emerging plant growth is juicy and abundant with carbohydrates. Mealybugs look like white, cottony patches and are disgusting to deal with, as their soft bodies smear with any pressure. Ants are a canary in the coal mine of sorts, usually indicating the presence of other pests that they are farming. Ants chaperone mealybug and aphid colonies, and they eat the other insects' sticky secretions.

For pest control, start with the most benign treatment first rather than unloading the big guns. Aphids, mealybugs, and ants can be blasted off with a jet of water to break up the infestation. A few treatments of 70 percent isopropyl alcohol applied with a spray bottle can be effective at killing any remaining mealybugs and aphids. Place ant baits close to affected plants, or spread diatomaceous earth on the soil in dry conditions.

More serious predators include agave snout weevil and aloe mite; a plant infested by either may need to be removed from the garden. The snout weevil is a small, black beetle that is problematic in Mexico, where tequila cultivation is widespread. Unfortunately, it is spreading its domain rapidly into California and the American Southwest. It tunnels into the core of the agave, laying eggs that hatch and eat the fleshy core from the inside out. If you find an agave whose leaves look wilted and possibly cocked sideways, this could indicate either a gopher attack or a dastardly weevil infestation. I don't advocate using chemical pesticides, and there is no organic treatment that will eradicate the weevil, so munched plants should be removed and disposed of.

Aloe mite is another serious pest that is also very difficult to treat. These tiny mites feast on aloe leaves and flowers, producing warty, tumorous, lumpy growths—a sort of aloe cancer. The deformed growth is irreparable, so it's best to remove and dispose of heavily colonized plants so the mites don't spread to other plants. Systemic pesticides have been used to control these insects, but these inorganic chemicals have been shown to appear in the flowers of the plant, toxifying the nectar that hummingbirds, bees, and other pollinators rely on as a food source. I've found some aloes to be mite-resistant—*A. taurii*, *A.* 'Moonglow', *A. barberae*, *A.* 'Hercules', *A. rubroviolacea*, *A. dorotheae*, and *A. striata*—and they show only occasional leaf scarring with limited flower distortion. If much of the aloe looks distressed, however, its best to remove the plant, let the area rest for a bit, and start over.

Gophers are the last scourge of the garden worth mentioning. They have a particular affinity for agaves (maybe gophers like tequila?). My garden is filled with various species, and I've witnessed a gopher tunnel 20 feet across the garden to pop up right beside a targeted agave. Gophers must have finely tuned agave radar, because all the other plants in this guy's tunneling path were completely uninteresting. The carbohydrate-rich core of the agave is the source of mescal, tequila, nectar, and other sweet concoctions, so the gopher's preference is understandable. To prevent gophers from devouring a plant from the ground up, you can use premade wire baskets, or make your own with aviary wire. Place the basket in the hole before planting to protect the roots from gopher boring. If you live in gopher country, an attack on your garden is not an *if*, but a *when*, so be prepared. As professional landscapers, we use root cages under every plant we sink in the ground, even if clients haven't witnessed gophers. Once you plant a new landscape, the bait is set, and it's only a matter of time before the invasion is on and you're losing plants like carrots in a Bugs Bunny episode. Do yourself a favor and use protective cages.

Bee mindful of avoiding chemicals to preserve our pollinators.

Weeds—Will They Ever Cease?

Although it's difficult to rationalize the value of garden pests, weeds do have the worthy job of stabilizing soil to prevent erosion. When the ground is disturbed by natural or manmade causes, weeds are the pioneers that tame the open territory, paving the way for other longer lived settlers to arrive. If we don't colonize our plots with choice plants, the weeds will have their way, making sure the earth keeps hold of her precious soil.

Weeds present the biggest challenge during the first year of any new garden. Seeds have been stirred up, watered, and enriched with compost, which creates ideal conditions for everything to boom indiscriminately. If you can maintain short, weekly weeding sessions, knocking out certain areas each time, weed seedlings tend to be small and are easy to pull. Reframe your perspective and treat a fifteen-minute weeding session as peaceful time grooming your new haven, or throw on some headphones with motivating music if birdsong doesn't move you.

My belief is that weeds keep us from getting complacent, both physically and mentally. Crouching and kneeling with a straight back are healthy ancestral movements, and they help you see differently, close to ground level. After the first year, the reactive weed growth will taper off, and the need to pull will be less frequent. Although weeds are a fact of life that no amount of landscape fabric, vinegar, or lemon oil can banish forever, you can use a few strategies to keep them at a threshold.

Be a water miser. Undesirable plants, like most others, need water to flourish, so try to limit watering only to cultivated areas; this will discourage weeds from sprouting in peripheral areas. Sprinklers spray water indiscriminately over larger areas, so avoid using them if possible, unless you have a very densely planted space. Drip or point source emitters distribute water only at the root balls of garden plants where it's needed, making them highly efficient with targeted irrigation. Hand-watering with a wand that diffuses the spray into a soft shower is also efficient if you have time and develop your technique. Manual watering can be relaxing if you don't have a large space, and it offers you a chance to make a connection with the plants in your garden.

Mulch, mulch, and mulch again. One of the gardener's greatest allies, a thick, 2 to 4-inch mulch layer blocks weed seeds from getting the sunlight that inspires germination. No sun equals no fun for weeds. The few weeds that are able to push through a heavy mulch layer are weakened and usually can be pulled out easily. Woodchip mulch slowly breaks down to feed the soil, which is a great benefit, but you'll need to reapply it every two years to maintain a depth it requires to continue its work as a weed barrier. Gravel mulches don't break down, but they can disperse in time and settle into the soil, so you'll need to reapply gravel every four to six years as an effective barrier and to keep beds looking tidy.

Don't disturb the ground any more than needed. Weeds get shaken out of bed with commotion, so keep them sleeping by letting them be. Tilling areas mechanically excites legions of weed seeds and disrupts soil structure. To prevent much unneeded work, loosen soil only in the areas in which you want to plant, and let that be it.

Keep a few specific weeding tools in the toolshed to help you stay ahead of oxalis, dandelions, and other noxious weeds. Like watering, weeding is an art, and having the right paintbrush for both broad strokes and fine details leverages your craft. Many Japanese companies excel at making fine tools for almost any gardening motion.

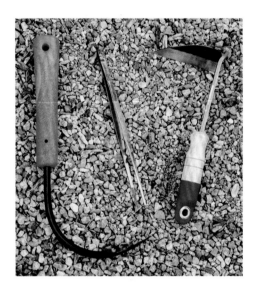

- For tough tap-rooted customers such as dandelions and thistles, the mighty, blue-handled CobraHead weeder (pictured, left) is unmatched. Its narrow head pierces through heavy clay, and the curved handle provides good leverage to pry out deep roots. The slender blade gets into tight spots around spiny succulents, where a trowel or bare hand is too clumsy. Long-handled versions of up to 60 inches enable you to stand up if you're not able to kneel.

- Long-handled metal tweezers (pictured, center, and on page 152), often used for reptile feeding or fish tanks, make the best tools for detail weeding in spiny territory. Oxalis in its many forms is gardener enemy number one and will quickly become your nemesis if you let it take control. Creeping wood sorrel and common yellow oxalis are the worst offenders in cactus and succulent beds, where they spread invasively by explosive seed pods that rupture and shoot seeds in every direction. They have an uncanny ability to root themselves in the tightest crevices between spines and sharp leaves, where it's nearly impossible to extract with spine-sensitive fingers. Use long-handled tweezers to reach precisely into the spiny zone, to pull out the brittle stems, usually in pieces. Regularly sold in sets, a range of 8- to 12-inch models provide good reach and dexterity for chasing invaders.

- Japanese garden hoes, such as my favorite lightweight Nejiri Gama Hoe (pictured on page 151, right), are made of hardened steel, and sport a thin, tapering blade pitched at a perfect angle for surface weeding. Its thin edge is razor-sharp and slices through weed stems without disturbing deeper weed seeds in the soil. Turn it sideways and use its pointed tip to cultivate in small areas between leaves or tightly spaced plants.

The moral of the story: Weeds test your patience. Move with slow perseverance and you can beat them, for the time being.

Succulent Gardening Gear

I have come to appreciate quality tools while working with the specific needs of succulents. Being a plant aficionado and landscaper for the past fifteen years, I've run through plenty of uninspiring tools—some that didn't even last a few hours in the field! Going cheap is actually expensive. Make it a point to seek out well-designed, high-quality tools that enhance your gardening superpowers. Quality gear gets you excited for your craft and pays dividends many times over in the long run. You'll find plenty of instruments to fill up your garden shed if you're a tool hound, but the focus here is on quality tools for weeding, digging, and pruning—our primary objectives in honing a succulent landscape.

SHARP PRUNERS FOR SHARP PLANTS

A good set of pruners is your best ally in the garden. I still use my original left-handed Felco F-9 pruners that were issued to me when I began school at the New York Botanical Garden. They're nineteen years old and still continue to slice with ease.

Swiss-made Felco pruners (pictured in bottom right of photo) are ideal for many gardeners: they feel good in the hand and cut even fibrous agave and yucca leaves readily. The bright red handles stand out well for visibility when you misplace them, though you should always use a holster or scabbard to keep them protected and at the ready. Models range from versions intended for small hands, to those created for lefties, plus ergonomic models and two-handed models that function like small loppers. And you will need only one pair in your lifetime, because replacement parts are readily available and every piece is changeable on most models. I replace the blade on mine every few years, after nicks from rocks, roots, and hard materials make them difficult to keep sharp. (I know they're supposed to be used only for above-ground plant material, but when they're at your side in a holster, it's way too easy to use them to tackle bigger wires and roots and to slice open bags of potting soil.) Bottom line, Felco pruners are built for abuse, and for about $50, they are worth their weight in gold. Don't go into the back yard without them!

There are definitely other quality pruner brands, with Bahco and Tobisho (pictured in center right of photo) worth naming.

A selection of pruners, plus some sharpeners (see page 156)

DIGGING IN

Shoveling may seem like a national pastime for most gardeners, as job number one often involves moving dirt. Even for small projects, when you're building berms, installing irrigation, or placing boulders, you'll often need to relocate a surprising amount of soil. A good shovel feels like a natural extension of your body and helps you maintain your posture as you use it. Shovel and spade design has come a long way, and shovels are designed to serve many distinct purposes. Having a variety of shovels in your arsenal is as important as having proper footwear for skiing, hiking, and going to the beach. Here I review a few essential diggers that will become close friends, offering you the most gain and least strain.

It's difficult to find a solid wooden-handled shovel these days. Hooray for that! Though I'm a fan of well-crafted traditional materials, solid hickory handles can't hold a candle to the flex and torque strength of metal or fiberglass when dealing with tough soil conditions. An ideal combination for everyday digging is a basic fiberglass/wood shaft combination with a rounded tip, rather than a handle grip on the end. The wooden core offers great shock absorption, and the fiberglass shell makes it rot-proof and flexible. As for blades, flat shovels are best for creating a clean line along bed edges, transferring gravel, and scooping large quantities of mulch off flat surfaces.

Bully Tools makes a good model that strikes a balance between strength and weight. My landscaping company and I have yet to break one of these shovels.

All-steel nursery spades (with blades welded onto the handle) are the Swiss Army knives of shovels and can be used as effective pry bars, root assassins, and transplanters all in one. You can plunge the long blade deep into the earth to slice tough roots and get under big, established root balls. The heavier weight of this shovel gives you the force you need to push through stubborn materials, and once there, you can use the shovel as leverage to pry against and loosen heavy clay, a boulder, or whatever else stands in your way. At around seven pounds, these shovels are not for

ABOVE, LEFT TO RIGHT: Drainspade, steel nursery spade, short-handled Radius transplanter, fiberglass shovel

OPPOSITE: A specimen Marina strawberry tree (*Arbutus* 'Marina') with shade-tolerant agaves and aeoniums.

everyday light work and will give you a nice heart-pumping workout. Costing around $100, they are an investment, but you will be able to pass on this sturdy tool to the next generation of gardeners. The line of steel shovels from the King of Spades from W. W. Manufacturing Co. are fine digging tools.

Try several other good small shovels to round out your assembly. The slender and longer bladed drain spade is helpful for getting into tight areas and for digging trenches. A short-handled spade is great when you need more precise control and for digging from your knees, as is a transplanting shovel with a short handle and tapered blade. The design of this shovel gives good leverage for breaking up dense soil and loosening root balls for transplanting. The small shovels from Radius Garden are particularly useful, with rounded shafts that provide a good grip in any position while kneeling. They are made of stainless steel to boot! Like a pair of shoes, heft a few models in the store before buying to get the best weight and feel for your frame.

TOOL CARE

Just as chefs strive to keep their knives in top shape, if you give your precious tools a little love, they will have a long, useful life. Always clean any sticky soil off hand tools and shovels after using them, and oil them in the off-season to prevent corrosion. Clean off sticky plant resins with alcohol after every few uses, and lightly oil pruner and other tool joints every couple of months to keep parts gliding freely.

Many sharpening implements are available to help you keep a prime edge on your shears. Your shears carry the lion's share of the work, and it's simple to keep them slicing like a samurai. A really dull blade is much harder to sharpen than one that's been tuned up regularly, and it takes less than a minute to hone your garden cutlass if you do it regularly.

Corona AC 8300 (pictured on page 153, lower left) is a slender, 5-inch carbon file that fits in your pocket and brings a fresh blade edge with a few passes. For about $9, this powerhouse works wonders for sharpening loppers, scissors, kitchen knives, and the edge on your spade. Sharpening the edge of a digging spade every so often makes a remarkable difference in its ability to cut through roots and dense soil. For a detailed edge, the Felco Istor I-20 Duplex Sharpener (pictured on page 153, upper right) is a multipurpose sharpener with a carbon file for quick sharpening and a dual-sided course/fine diamond grinder for fine-tuning. Slightly bigger than the Corona, it offers greater versatility in sharpening light-duty tools and heavier blades of axes and loppers. The diamond grinder end of the tool takes off burrs and restores the cutting surface back to original condition.

CHAPTER 8

Propagation

Having cultivated an array of woody and herbaceous plants, I would recognize succulents as the most altruistic of the plant kingdom. Every plant creates fruit, flowers, and foliage in some fashion, but succulents are known philanthropists that offer more goodwill at multiple junctures of maturity. Not content to create new colonies only by seed, most succulents are masters of asexual propagation (by cuttings). Most species from the Crassula (Crassulaceae) family (see chapter 3, Saucers, Platters, and Pinwheels) can be propagated using a single leaf or stem cutting. Aloes and agaves prefer to celebrate reproduction via plantlets, the basal offsets and bulbils that are nursed by the mother plant until they can root on their own.

This ease of propagation is a great boon for those of you just joining the succulent pursuit, as you can start with a handful of plants and expand your collection without going broke. I find that plants provide a great platform for befriending a neighbor or meeting like-minded people from the local chapter of the Cactus and Succulent Society. Those with established collections usually run out of room in time and are happy to share new offsets. Through propagation, the succulent movement is actively birthing a pay-it-forward community!

Succulents come well-equipped to re-create themselves from the smallest speck of tissue. For non-succulent plants, vegetative cuttings take precise monitoring of humidity, soil moisture, and temperature to stimulate root formation and the beginnings of a new plant. However, desiccation and rot are common in herbaceous plants, and rooting percentages are far from 100 percent. Most of those fussy plants can be thrown out the window, because succulents have a different modus operandi. With onboard hydration and an iron will to survive, succulents often produce roots on their own without us intervening. In the succulent camp, the easiest varieties to propagate are in the Crassulaceae family: echeverias, aeoniums, sedums, kalanchoes, cotyledons, crassulas, graptopetalums, and sempervivums. These plants just want to reproduce and will be darned if you stand in their way!

Mexican snowball (*Echeveria elegans*)

Propagating succulents is just plain fun. Watching new plants multiply from a tiny echeveria leaf or a leggy sedum stem gives you a delightful sense of accomplishment. Propagating succulents does not involve advanced techniques reserved for greenhouse and nursery specialists; anyone with a few plants and a hint of curiosity can successfully propagate these plants. Succulent swaps are common in gardening circles, where people trade rooted cuttings and other starts. Meetups are a fun way to meet new people with plant inclinations, learn new hacks, and grow your collection.

Stem Cuttings

Many sedums, aeoniums, kalanchoes, and echeverias are known for getting leggy and can benefit from an annual renewal pruning. Their upper growth makes ideal material for stem cuttings. After you cut back the top half or third of the plant, the remaining base plant will regenerate with access to sunlight. This hardy new cutting will already have its top rosette of leaves intact. (Any sections taken from farther down the stem will root equally as well; they just don't look as pretty initially.) Stem propagation is also an easy way to create new aloes, yuccas, euphorbias, and other trunking succulents.

1. Cut off the top half or third of the existing plant.

2. Gently remove each leaf from the bottom third of the cutting.

3. Let the cutting rest in part shade for a week, not planted in soil, so it can callous the wound where it formerly met the stem. If you have a heavy head cutting with a larger mass of leaves, such as from a fan aloe, give the larger stem a few weeks to callous before potting.

4. After the wound has healed over, sink the bottom $1/4$ of the stem into moistened planting mix (use cactus mix or add perlite to commercial potting soil in a 50/50 mix). If you have a heavy head cutting, lean the plant against a few rocks or a stake in the potting mix to prop it up while it grows roots.

5. For small cuttings, keep the mix slightly moist by using a spray bottle or diffused nozzle once a week. The plant will draw much of the water it needs from its own reserves in the rooting phase. For large cuttings, water only once a week, or less, with a hose or watering can to provide time for the soil to dry between waterings. If the planting mix is too heavy or you overwater, you can kill the cutting.

6. Leave the potted cuttings in part shade for a few weeks in moist soil as the roots form. It's natural for cuttings to look stressed or limp for the first week or two, but you can tell the minute roots begin taking hold because the cuttings will plump up and color up like they've been resuscitated.

Propagating Coppertone stonecrop (*Sedum nussbaumerianum* 'Coppertone') by stem and leaf cutting, with the final picture showing the plantlets formed by each leaf.

Leaf Cuttings

You can create a new plant by using leaf cuttings of leafy succulents such as sedums and echeverias. Here's how to create a cutting:

1. Gently bend a leaf side-to-side until it makes a clean break off the stem. If the leaf tears, it has less chance of rooting, so do this part carefully to keep the base of the leaf intact.

2. Once the leaf is removed, allow the small, open wound at the end of the leaf to heal over, as with a stem cutting. Set the leaf cuttings in a partly shaded area out of direct sun for a few days to enable the wound to callous.

3. Once the wound looks shriveled and sealed, place each leaf in a container on top of cactus mix, preferably in a windowsill with a few hours of morning sun. Leaves don't need to be pressed into the mix at this point.

4. Mist the leaves every few days with a spray bottle, moistening the soil, and within a few weeks, clusters of tiny, white roots will appear as the leaves search for a new water source.

5. Keep misting, and small plantlets will appear, with the roots ready to brave the new world. At this stage, press the leaves and the roots into the soil so they can develop further. Once underground, the parent leaves will wither away on their own as the plants take off.

6. Again, saturating the soil too often will rot the youngsters at this early stage, so water only once a week, or less, depending on conditions, providing time for the soil to dry between waterings.

Offsets

Offsets, aka pups, are another specialized method of reproduction used by many agaves and rosette species that form plant colonies. Agaves produce prolific offsets, with some species, such as the American century plant (*Agave americana*) and sisal, or hemp, agave (*A. sisalana*), producing large, lethal stands known to contain missing livestock. These widespread century plants are too large and aggressive to use in most residential landscapes, but there are many better behaving agaves, such as those detailed in chapter 5, The Spiny Side. Although some agave species can grow out of control, responsible pupping is a positive trait in smaller agaves whose pups develop close to the mother plant.

This pupping growth pattern is also the norm for hens and chicks (*Echeveria* and *Sempervivum* species), with the mother hen being the main rosette that bears a brood of many small chick plantlets (see photo, page 52). Offsets are vegetative clones—exact reproductions of the mother plant—that create a homogenous colony, spreading over time without relying on seed. Propagation by offsets is so successful because the mother plant has done all the work, producing a fully viable rooted plant that's ready to rock.

Propagating Mexican snowball (*Echeveria elegans*) by offsets.

Offsets are connected to the parent plant by ropey runners (especially in agaves) that function like an umbilical cord. The pups are fed and watered by the mother plant as long as they are connected. Once the offset produces roots, it becomes a satellite plant—this is the prime time to harvest offsets, as rooting has begun, but plants aren't too well developed. Here's how to propagate with an offset:

1. Pups start as new rosettes that are tightly attached to mother stem, elongating as they mature.

2. Once a pup stem has extended a few inches from the mother, a cluster of roots will often appear on their own. At this point, gently wiggle the pup's stem from the mother, or cut it off with clean pruning shears. Then dig around the pup to lift any tiny roots that have initiated.

3. Let the wound callous for a few days.

4. Add the plantlet directly to the garden or soil mix in a container.

Bulbils

Never one to be shy, agaves have another reproductive trick up their sleeves beyond seeds and pups. Once the agave flowers have matured, tiny plantlets form in the nodes (armpits) of the flower stalk in a few noted species, such as foxtail agave (*Agave attenuata*), smooth agave (*A. desmetiana*), octopus agave (*A. vilmoriniana*), and the gypsum century plant (*A. gypsophila*).

Also known as bulbils, these miniature agave plants resemble tiny pineapples, with a curvy shape and a spray of leaves on top. The key to harvesting these is to let the bloom stalk fully mature so all remaining stored sugars in the mother are pumped into this new generation, resulting in a prime starter plant. When the bulbil is allowed to mature on the bloom stalk, a few roots form, indicating that they are ready to go. Gently twist them from the bloom stalk, and place the tiny plants in cactus mix for a few months to build more roots. Bulbils, including select variegated cultivars, are clones and retain their parent's distinct traits.

Agave gypsophila bulbils forming.

COLD-HARDY SUCCULENTS

	AGAVE	YUCCA
ZONE 8 (10 TO 20°F)	Cabbage head agave (*A. parrasana*) Ocahui agave (*A. ocahui*) Quadricolor century plant (*A. lophantha* 'Quadricolor') Mountain agave (*A. montana*)	Blue Boy yucca (*Y. desmetiana* 'Blue Boy')
ZONE 7 (0 TO 10°F)	Squid agave (*A. bracteosa*) Golden-flowered century plant (*A. chrysantha*) Whale's tongue agave (*A. ovatifolia*) King Ferdinand century plant (*A. nickelsiae*) Queen Victoria agave (*A. victoriae-reginae*) Narrow-leaf century plant (*A. striata*) Jaws agave (*A. gentryi* 'Jaws') Parry's agave (*A. parryi*)	Our Lord's candle (*Y. whipplei*, aka *Hesperoyucca whipplei*) Bright Star yucca (*Yucca* Bright Star) Spanish dagger (*Y. aloifolia*)
ZONE 6 (-10 TO 0°F)	Shin daggers (*A. lechuguilla*) Havard's century plant (*A. havardiana*) Utah agave (*A. utahensis*)	Beaked yucca (*Y. rostrata*) Joshua tree (*Y. brevifolia*)
ZONE 5 (-20 TO -10°F)	Fairy-ring agave (*A. toumeyana* var. *bella*)	Red yucca (*Hesperaloe parvifolia*) Color Guard yucca (*Y. filamentosa* 'Colorguard') Soapweed (*Y. glauca*) Banana yucca (*Y. baccata*)

	CACTI	LEAFY SUCCULENTS
ZONE 8 (10 TO 20°F)	San Pedro cactus (*Echinopsis pachinoi*) Silver torch (*Cleistocactus strausii*)	All leafy succulents listed below under Zones 7, 6, and 5 also do well in Zone 8
ZONE 7 (0 TO 10°F)	Fishhook barrel cactus (*Ferocactus wislizeni*) Texas barrel cactus (*F. hamatacanthus*) Old man of the mountain (*Oreocerus* spp.) Spineless prickly pear (*Opuntia cacanapa* 'Ellisiana') Santa Rita prickly pear (*O. santa-rita* aka *O. violaea* var. *santa-rita*)	Lesser Mexican stonecrop (*Sedum confusum*)
ZONE 6 (-10 TO 0°F)	All cacti listed below under Zone 5 also do well in Zone 6	*Delosperma* Hotcakes series Broadleaf stonecrop (*Sedum spathulifolium*)
ZONE 5 (-20 TO -10°F)	Claret cup cactus (*Echinocereus triglochidiatus*) Lace hedgehog cactus (*E. reichenbachii*) Viviparous foxtail cactus (*Escobaria vivipara* var. *rosea*) Beavertail prickly pear (*Opuntia basilaris*) Dark Knight prickly pear (*O. polyacantha* 'Dark Knight')	Cooper's ice plant (*Delosperma cooperi*) Fire Spinner ice plant (*D.* 'Fire Spinner') All *Jovibarba* and *Sempervivum* species October daphne (*Sedum sieboldii*) Broadleaf stonecrop (*S. spathufolium*) Russian stonecrop (*S. kamtschaticum*) Corsican stonecrop (*S. dasyphyllum*) Oregon stonecrop (*S. oreganum*)

RESOURCES

Retail Nurseries

Some of these growers also offer mail-order.

ARIZONA

B & B Cactus Farm
11550 E Speedway Boulevard, Tucson
bandbcactus.com
(502) 721-4687

CALIFORNIA

Aloes in Wonderland
114 Conejo Road, Santa Barbara
aloesinwonderland.com
(805) 965-0895

Desert Theater Nursery
9655 Kiwi Meadow Lane, Escondido
deserttheater.com
(760) 594-2330

Flora Grubb Gardens
1634 Jerrold Avenue, San Francisco
floragrubb.com
(415) 626-7256

Grow Nursery
2024 Main Street, Cambria
grownursery.com
(805) 924-1340

Solana Succulents
355 N. Highway 101, Solana Beach
solanasucculents.com
(858) 259-4568

Succulent Gardens
2133 Elkhorn Road, Castroville
sgplants.com
(831) 632-0482

Waterwise Botanicals
32151 Old Highway 395, Bonsall
waterwisebotanicals.com
(760) 728-2641

FLORIDA

Florida Cactus Inc.
2542 Peterson Road, Apopka
floridacactus.com
(407) 886-1833

Paradise Found Nursery
3570 Tallevast Road, Sarasota
paradisefoundnursery.com
(540) 229-1997

Kalanchoe 'Oak Leaf' and *Agave* 'Blue Flame'

NORTH CAROLINA

Plant Delights Nursery, Inc.
9241 Sauls Road, Raleigh
plantdelights.com
(919) 772-4794

OHIO

Groovy Plants Ranch
4140 County Road 15, Marengo
groovyplantsranch.com
(740) 675-2681

OKLAHOMA

J & J Cactus and Succulents
600 N. Pine Street, Midwest City
jjcactus-succulents.net
(405) 737-1831

OREGON

SMG succulents
Eagle Creek
smgsucculents.com
(503) 637-3585

TEXAS

Cactus King
7900 I-45 North, Houston
thecactusking.com
(281) 591-8833

East Austin Succulents
801 Tillery Street, Austin
eastaustinsucculents.com
(512) 701-3448

Mail-Order Nurseries

UNITED STATES

Cold Hardy Cactus
coldhardycactus.com

Greg Starr's Nursery
starr-nursery.com

High Country Gardens
highcountrygardens.com

Mountain Crest Gardens
mountaincrestgardens.com

Plant Delights Nursery
plantdelights.com

Steve Super Gardens
stevesupergardens.com

SOUTH AFRICA

Silverhill Seeds
silverhillseeds.co.za

Botanical Gardens

ARIZONA

Desert Botanical Garden
1201 N. Galvin Parkway, Phoenix
dbg.org
(480) 941-1225

CALIFORNIA

Ganna Walska Lotusland
Cold Spring Road, Montecito
lotusland.org
(805) 969-9990

Huntington Botanical Gardens
1151 Oxford Road, San Marino
huntington.org
(626) 405-2100

Ruth Bancroft Garden
1552 Bancroft Road, Walnut Creek
ruthbancroftgarden.org
(925) 944-9352

COLORADO

Denver Botanic Gardens
1007 York Street, Denver
botanicgardens.org
(720) 865-3500

NEVADA

Ethel M Botanical Cactus Garden
2 Cactus Garden Drive, Henderson
ethelm.com/botanical-cactus-garden
(800) 438-4356

NEW MEXICO

Desert Conservancy at the ABQ BioPark Botanic Garden
2601 Central Avenue NW, Albuquerque
cabq.gov/culturalservices/biopark/
garden
(505) 768-2000

NEW YORK

New York Botanical Garden
2900 Southern Boulevard, Bronx
nybg.org
(718) 817-8700

UTAH

Ogden Botanical Garden
1750 Monroe Blvd, Ogden
ogdenbotanicalgardens.org
(801) 399-8080

WISCONSIN

Mitchell Park Horticultural Conservatory
524 S. Layton Blvd, Milwaukee
milwaukeedomes.org
(414) 257-5600

Garden Tool Suppliers

A. M. Leonard Horticultural Tool & Supply Company
amleo.com

Gardeners Supply Company
gardeners.com

Hida Tool & Hardware
hidatool.com

Niwaki
niwaki.com

W. W. Manufacturing Company
wwmfg.com

ACKNOWLEDGMENTS

How could I not give thanks to everyone who has made an impact on me up until this very moment? Forces both seen and unseen have proven instrumental in preparing me for the opportunity of writing a book about the wonders of succulent plants. For these reasons, I have infinite gratitude for family, friends, and teachers of all walks who have generously shared their time and wisdom. Please know that any names not included in this brief acknowledgment are due to lack of space and not lack of appreciation.

Over the years, I've had the great fortune of being in the grace of many individuals who have cultivated a strong connection with the earth. Ecologists, botanists, dirt gardeners, and glasshouse horticulturists were equal allies in shaping my holistic understanding of the plant kingdom. My early days of sowing seed crops barefoot in the back yard with my parents showed me where food truly came from. Working with landscape designers in the Appalachian Mountains demonstrated how to view landscape development as a dynamic art form—impressing on me that the values of quality craftsmanship and having fun with your trade are equally important. Larry Santoyo of Earthflow Designs honed my ability of natural pattern recognition and showed me how we can integrate appropriate technology with the forces of wind, water, sun, and earth to solve the greatest problems humans face.

My specialized training at the New York Botanical Garden was a renaissance experience, blowing off the doors to a worldwide spectrum of horticulture. NYBG's entire team of gardeners, propagators, researchers, and teachers was a continual inspiration to dig deeper into the 200-acre living laboratory that surrounded us. I credit these years of intense study at NYBG as formative—developing my seedling inclinations into a solid trunk (body) of working knowledge. Much gratitude to my then classmate, now friend and landscape design partner, Kaveh Maguire, for his encouragement to flee the East Coast and spend our internship at Mendocino Coast Botanical Gardens. California has kept me in awe ever since.

Big high-five to friend, collaborator, and fellow landscape designer Nick Wilkinson of Botanica Nova and Grow Nursery, whose garden design is pictured on page 15. A succulent ninja of the tenth degree, Nick was the first plant nut I met in San Luis Obispo County. Always willing to share a signature knowledge of oddball plants, art, and artifacts, his keen eye and effervescent presence make great things happen. I'd also like to thank Fortini Landscapes, who designed the garden on page 107, and Rhythm and Roots Landscaping, whose garden design is featured on page 129.

The eclectic plant quiver I draw from owes a huge debt to the skilled growers of San Luis Obispo County. Native Sons Nursery, Growing Grounds Nursery, West Covina Nurseries, and Clearwater Color Nursery produce consistent quality plants and bring new and outstanding varieties that enable us to continue pushing limits of drought tolerance and adaptability. San Marcos Growers in Santa Barbara is a haven for distinctive plants from all over the world. I feel privileged to work with these excellent growers that enable an adventurous plant palette.

My gracious editor, Lisa Regul, deserves great commendation for keeping me in the game when everything else fell out! Your coaching

Fan aloe (*Aloe plicatilis*)

and collaborative vision has supported this work to reach its potential. Thanks to designer Chloe Rawlins and production manager Jane Chinn at Ten Speed Press. Much gratitude to my tireless photographer and friend, Dan Kuras, for capturing the glowing imagery that decorates these pages. He never refused, even as I promised just one more garden after the sun had left us and the winds howled. Special thanks to Jeff Chemnick of Aloes in Wonderland for allowing us to photograph his superb collection on multiple occasions. Stacy Peralta's insight has been invaluable in tracking down the IDs of many mystery aloes.

This book would have been impossible without the caring support and dedication of my lovely wife, Maggie Ragatz. The need for keeping my wild ideas and equally feral grammar in check cannot be overestimated. Giving me the time of so many nights and weekends fostered the writing to its completion.

ABOUT THE AUTHOR

Gabriel Frank is a devout advocate for all things green and growing. He is the head dirt-monger at Gardens by Gabriel, Inc., a licensed landscape design + build firm on the Central Coast of California. He and his team enjoy working with clients to create one-of-a-kind outdoor living environments that infuse water-wise beauty with artistic flair. Outside of building landscapes for others, he can be found cultivating edibles, succulents, and Mediterranean natives in his own home demonstration garden. A father of two young girls, he enjoys peddling Hannah and Clara on their orange e-bike through the hills of Morro Bay.

INDEX

A

Acanthus mollis (bear's breech), 127

Adenanthos sericeus (woolly bush), 35

Aeonium, 42–44

A. canariensis (giant velvet rose aeonium), 19, 42

A. 'Cyclops' (giant red aeonium), 44, 129

A. 'Kiwi' (Kiwi aeonium), 35, 42, 44

A. 'Pseudotabuliforme' (green platters), 44, 55

A. 'Sunburst', viii, 8

A. undulatum (saucer plant), 41, 43

A. urbicum (dinner plate aeonium), 11

A. 'Voodoo', 44

A. 'Zwartkop' (black rose aeonium), 19, 44

African candelabra (*Euphorbia ammak*), 109

African milk barrel (*Euphorbia horrida*), 109

Afterglow echeveria (*Echeveria* 'Afterglow'), 31, 50, 53, 57

Agastache (hyssop), 120

Agave
  characteristics of, 84
  cold-hardy, 166
  midsize, 88–89
  small, 84–87

A. americana (American century plant), 163

A. attenuata (foxtail agave), 164

A. attenuata 'Ray of Light' (Ray of Light century plant), 127, 129

A. 'Blue Flame' (Blue Flame century plant), 4, 117, 129, 130, 139, 169

A. 'Blue Glow' (Blue Glow agave), 85, 91, 104, 107, 139

A. bracteosa (squid agave), 85, 166

A. chazaroi, 62, 121

A. chrysantha (golden-flowered century plant), 166

A. desmetiana (smooth agave), 89, 117, 164

A. desmetiana 'Variegata', 2

A. filifera (thread agave), 91

A. geminiflora (twin-flowered agave), 4, 86

A. gentryi 'Jaws' (Jaws agave), 91, 166

A. gypsophila (gypsum century plant), 127, 164, 165

A. havardiana (Havard's century plant), 166

A. 'Kissho Kan', 86–87, 133

A. lechuguilla (shin daggers), 166

A. lopahanta 'Quadricolor' (Quadricolor century plant), 79, 80, 166

A. montana (mountain agave), 77, 166

A. 'Mr. Ripple', 91

A. nickelsiae (King Ferdinand century plant), 166

A. ocahui (Ocahui agave), 84–85, 166

A. oteroi 'Felipe Otero' (Sierra Mixteca agave), 79, 80

A. ovatifolia (whale's tongue agave), 14, 91, 166

A. parrasana (cabbage head agave), 166

A. parryi (Parry's agave), viii, 107, 109, 114, 166

A. potatorum (butterfly agave), 86–87

A. sisalana (sisal agave), 163

agave snout weevil, 148–49

A. striata (narrow-leaf century plant), 166

A. toumeyana var. *bella* (fairy-ring agave), 166

A. utahensis (Utah agave), 166

A. victoriae-reginae (Queen Victoria agave), 87, 133, 166

A. vilmoriniana (octopus agave), 88–89, 164

Aloe
  breeders of, 60
  characteristics of, 59, 61
  clustering, 61, 72–75
  geographic distribution of, 61
  number of species of, 59
  single-trunk, 61, 70–72
  tree, 61, 64, 66–68

A. arborescens 'Spineless' (toothless torch aloe), 21

A. barberae (giant tree aloe, aka *Aloidendron barberae*), 62, 64, 66, 149

A. 'Blue Elf' (Blue Elf aloe), 77, 114

A. bracteosa (spider aloe), 74

A. cameronii (red aloe), 77

A. capitata, 68

A. chabaudii (Dwala aloe), 68, 77

A. 'Cynthia Giddy', 73

A. dichotoma (quiver tree, aka *Aloidendron dichotoma*), 21, 64, 67

A. dorotheae (sunset aloe), 72–73, 75, 149

A. elegans (palmbob aloe), 8, 68

A. excelsa (Zimbabwe aloe), vii, 60, 77

A. eximia, 68

A. ferox (bitter aloe), 68, 71

A. 'Hercules', 149

A. marlothii (mountain aloe), 59, 60, 70–71

A. marlothii x *excelsa*, 68

aloe mite, 148, 149

A. 'Moonglow' (Moonglow aloe), 62, 79, 80, 149

A. munchii (Chimanimani aloe), 21

A. plicatilis (fan aloe), 68, 114, 173

A. plurideus (French aloe), 21

A. pluridens (French aloe), 21

A. ramosissima (maiden's quiver tree), 77

A. 'Rooikappie', 73

A. rubroviolacea, 149

A. rupestris (bottlebrush aloe), 77
Aloes in Wonderland (garden
  project), 77
A. speciosa (tilt-head aloe), 68,
  71–72
A. spicata, 68
A. striata (coral aloe), viii, 73–74,
  115, 149
A. taurii (Bullock's bottle brush),
  62, 121, 149
A. thraskii (dune aloe), 139
A. tongaensis (Mozambique
  tree aloe, aka *Aloidendron
  tongaensis*), 64, 66
A. vanbalenii (Van Balen's aloe),
  74–75
A. vera, 26, 59
A. vilmoriniana (octopus aloe), 74
A. wickensii, 68
*Aloidendron barberae. See Aloe
  barberae*
A. dichotoma. See Aloe dichotoma
A. tongaensis. See Aloe tongaensis
amendments, 135–37
American century plant (*Agave
  americana*), 163
Anchor Bay ceanothus (*Ceanothus
  gloriosus* 'Anchor Bay'), 127
ants, 148
aphids, 148
Arbutus 'Marina' (Marina
  strawberry tree), 79,
  129, 155
Arctostaphylos insularis
  'Canyon Sparkles' (island
  mazanita), 127
areoles, 2, 94–95
Arizona barrel cactus. *See*
  fishhook barrel cactus
Ascot Rainbow spurge (*Euphorbia*
  'Ascot Rainbow'), 31
Asparagus densiflorus 'Myers'
  (foxtail fern), 11
Astelia nervosa (mountain
  astelia), 127
Avent, Tony, 8

B
Baja fairy duster (*Calliandra
  californica*), 117
ball cactus (*Parodia
  magnifica*), 104

banana yucca (*Yucca baccata*),
  91, 166
Barr, Claude, 8
beaked yucca (*Yucca rostrata*), 93,
  103, 166
beardtongue (*Penstemon*), 120–21
bear's breech (*Acanthus
  mollis*), 127
Beaucarnea 'Gold Star', 4
B. guatemalensis, 4
B. recurvata (ponytail palm), 109
beavertail prickly pear (*Opuntia
  basilaris*), 102, 167
Berlandier's sundrops (*Calylophus
  berlandieri*), 119
berms, 136–37
bitter aloe (*Aloe ferox*), 68, 71
black rose aeonium (*Aeonium
  'Zwartkop'*), 19, 44
Bleck, John, 60
Blue Boy yucca (*Yucca desmetiana
  'Blue Boy'*), 91, 115, 166
blue candle (*Myrtillocactus
  geometrizans*), 91, 109
blue chalk sticks (*Senecio
  mandraliscae*), 19, 25
Blue Elf aloe (*Aloe* 'Blue Elf'),
  77, 114
Blue Flame century plant (*Agave
  'Blue Flame'*), 4, 117, 129,
  130, 139, 169
Blue Glow agave (*Agave* 'Blue
  Glow'), 85, 91, 104, 107, 139
blue palo verde (*Parkinsonia
  florida*), 125
blue-skinned cactus
  (*Pilosocereus*), 97
Blue Spruce stonecrop (*Sedum
  reflexum* 'Blue Spruce'),
  21, 74
Bodhi Bowl (garden project), 35
botanical gardens, 170–71
bottlebrush aloe (*Aloe
  rupestris*), 77
bottle tree (*Brachychiton
  rupestris*), 77
Bouteloua dactyloides (buffalo
  grass), 101
Brachychiton rupestris (bottle
  tree), 77
bread palm (*Encephalartos*), 77

bright green dudleya (*Dudleya
  virens*), 47, 48
Bright Star yucca (*Yucca* Bright
  Star), 14, 24, 91, 115, 166
Brittle Star dyckia (*Dyckia* 'Brittle
  Star'), 37
Britton's dudleya (*Dudleya
  brittonii*), 45, 47
broadleaf stonecrop (*Sedum
  spathulifolium*), 7, 167
buffalo grass (*Bouteloua
  dactyloides*), 101
bulbils, 164–65
Bullock's bottle brush (*Aloe taurii*),
  62, 121, 149
bunny ears cactus (*Opuntia
  microdasys*), 101
butterfly agave (*Agave potatorum*),
  86–87

C
cabbage head agave (*Agave
  parrasana*), 166
cacti
  areoles and, 2, 94–95
  barrel, 103–4
  characteristics of, 94–95
  climate and, 97
  columnar, 95, 97, 100
  handling, 98
  number of species of, 95
  paddle, 101–2
  succulents vs., 2, 94
  See also individual species
Caesalpinia gilliesii (yellow bird of
  paradise), 118
C. pulcherrima (red bird of
  paradise), 118
California fan palm (*Washingtonia
  filifera*), 103
Calliandra californica (Baja fairy
  duster), 117
C. eriophylla (pink fairy
  duster), 117
Callistemon viminalis 'Slim' (Slim
  bottlebrush), 129
Calylophus berlandieri
  (Berlandier's sundrops), 119
C. hartwegii (Hartweg's
  sundrops), 125
Campfire plant (*Crassula capitella*
  'Campfire'), 31

candy barrel cactus. *See* fishhook barrel cactus

Canyon Prince wild rye (*Leymus condensatus* 'Canyon Prince'), 127

Carnegiea gigantea (saguaro cactus), 95

Ceanothus gloriosus 'Anchor Bay' (Anchor Bay ceanothus), 127

Cedros Island dudleya (*Dudleya pachyphytum*), 45, 48

century plant. *See Agave*

Cephalocereus senilis (old man cactus), 97

Cereus peruvianus f. *monstrose* (monstrose apple cactus), 2, 94

chalk dudleya (*Dudleya pulverulenta*), 44, 45, 46, 47, 146

Chemnick, Jeff, 77

chenille plant (*Echeveria pulvinata*), 14

Chimanimani aloe (*Aloe munchii*), 21

cholla (*Cylindropuntia*), 109

Christmas cactus (*Schlumbergera*), 94–95

claret cup cactus (*Echinocereus triglochidiatus*), 167

Cleistocactus strausii (silver torch cactus), 97, 167

climate, 6–8, 27, 146, 166–67

Color Guard yucca (*Yucca filamentosa* 'Colorguard'), 93, 166

companion plants, 122–23

compass barrel cactus (*Ferocactus cylindraceus*), 83

compost, 135–37

conebushes (*Leucadendron*), 62, 116–17

container gardens
  advantages of, 25–26, 28, 32
  in cold climates, 27
  containers for, 28, 29
  history of, 25
  plants for, 28, 31
  projects, 35, 37–38
  short-term, 26
  size of, 31
  watering, 31–32

contrast, 14

Cooper's ice plant (*Delosperma cooperi*), 167

copper spoons (*Kalanchoe orgyalis*), 28

Coppertone stonecrop (*Sedum nussbaumerianum* 'Coppertone'), 21, 31, 35, 73, 74, 161

Coprosma (mirror bush), 117

C. 'Fireburst' (Fireburst mirror plant), 129

C. repens 'Painter's Palette', 35

coral aloe (*Aloe striata*), viii, 73–74, 115, 149

Corsican stonecrop (*Sedum dasyphyllum*), 167

Cotyledon (pig's ear), 109

Crassula capitella 'Campfire' (Campfire plant), 31

C. ovata 'Hummel's Sunset' (Hummel's Sunset jade plant), 21

C. tetragona (miniature pine tree), 19

Cubic Frost echeveria (*Echeveria* 'Cubic Frost'), 57

Cylindropuntia (cholla), 109

D

Dark Knight prickly pear (*Opuntia polyacantha* 'Dark Knight'), 167

David Cumming graptoveria (*Graptoveria* 'David Cumming'), 37

Delosperma (ice plants), 7

D. cooperi (Cooper's ice plant), 167

D. 'Fire Spinner' (Fire Spinner ice plant), 73, 167

D. Hotcakes series, 167

dinner plate aeonium (*Aeonium urbicum*), 11

Discography (garden project), 37–38

Dondo echeveria (*Echeveria* 'Dondo'), 37, 41

Dracaena draco (dragon tree), 107

drainage, 136–37

Dudleya (live-forevers), 43, 44–48

D. brittonii (Britton's dudleya), 45, 47

D. caespitosa (sea lettuce dudleya), 47, 48

D. gnoma (munchkin dudleya), 48

D. greenei (Greene's dudleya), 48

D. pachyphytum (Cedros Island dudleya), 45, 48

D. pulverulenta (chalk dudleya), 44, 45, 46, 47, 146

D. virens (bright green dudleya), 47, 48

dune aloe (*Aloe thraskii*), 139

Dwala aloe (*Aloe chabaudii*), 68, 77

Dyckia 'Brittle Star' (Brittle Star dyckia), 37

Dymondia margaretae, 4

E

Echeveria 'Afterglow' (Afterglow echeveria), 31, 50, 53, 57

E. agavoides (lipstick echeveria), 50, 53, 121

E. 'Blue Curls', 50

E. cante (white cloud echeveria), 57

E. colorata 'Mexican Giant', 41, 50

E. 'Cubic Frost' (Cubic Frost echeveria), 57

E. 'Dick Wright', 50

E. 'Dondo' (Dondo echeveria), 37, 41

E. 'Doris Taylor', 50

E. 'Ebony', 48, 50, 53

E. (Mexican snowball), 35, 37, 41, 50, 53, 55, 57, 159, 163

E. 'Etna', 50

E. x *Imbricata*, 48

Echeveria Jewel Box (garden project), 57

E. 'Latte Rose' (Latte Rose echeveria), 50, 57

E. 'Lipstick', 4

E. 'Mauna Loa' (red frills echeveria), 57

E. 'Perle von Nurnberg', 25, 117

E. pulvinata (chenille plant), 14

E. 'Ruffles', 2

Echeverría y Godoy, Atanasio, 50

Echinocactus grusonii (golden barrel cactus), 103, 107, 109

Echinocereus, 8
E. *reichenbachii* (lace hedgehog cactus), 167
E. *triglochidiatus* (claret cup cactus), 167
Echinopsis (hedgehog cacti), 2
E. *huascha*, 91
E. *pachanoi* (San Pedro cactus), 6, 97, 100, 104, 109, 167
E. *spachiana* (golden torch), 109
elephant food (*Portulacaria afra* 'Aurea'), 31, 117
Encephalartos (bread palm), 77
E. *horridus*, vii
Erigonum grande var. *rubescens* (San Miguel Island buckwheat), 127
Escobaria, 8
E. *vivipara* var. *rosea* (viviparous foxtail cactus), 167
Euphorbia ammak (African candelabra), 109
E. 'Ascot Rainbow' (Ascot Rainbow spurge), 31
E. *horrida* (African milk barrel), 109
E. *resinifera* (Moroccan mound), 79, 80, 91
E. *tirucalli* 'Sticks on Fire' (fire sticks), 28, 75

F

fairy-ring agave (*Agave toumeyana* var. *bella*), 166
fan aloe (*Aloe plicatilis*), 68, 114, 173
feathery cassia (*Senna artemisioides*), 118
Ferocactus cylindraceus (compass barrel cactus), 83
F. *hamatacanthus* (Texas barrel cactus), 167
F. *wislizeni* (fishhook barrel cactus), 104, 167
fertilizers, 135
Fireburst mirror plant (*Coprosma* 'Fireburst'), 129
Fire Spinner ice plant (*Delosperma* 'Fire Spinner'), 73, 167
fire sticks (*Euphorbia tirucalli* 'Sticks on Fire'), 28, 75

fishhook barrel cactus (*Ferocactus wislizeni*), 104, 167
fish hooks (*Senecio radicans*), 31, 37
form, 14
foxtail agave (*Agave attenuata*), 164
foxtail fern (*Asparagus densiflorus* 'Myers'), 11
French aloe (*Aloe plurideus*), 21
frost cloth, 146, 148
fusion gardens
concept of, 111–12
flowers for, 119–23
garden projects for, 127, 129–30
shrubs for, 112–18, 122–23
trees for, 112, 122–23

G

garden design
contrast, 14
form, 14
rhythm, 4
scale, 62
for small spaces, 11–14, 16
texture, 14
garden projects
Aloes in Wonderland, 77
Bodhi Bowl, 35
Discography, 37–38
Echeveria Jewel Box, 57
Jurassic Hillside, 109
Moonlighting, 79–80
Pinwheel Hearts, 55
Restful Retreat, 129–30
Secret Passage, 19
Sleek Lines and Spines, 107
Welcome Home, 127
Gentry, Howard, 88
germander sage (*Salvia chamaedryoides*), 111
ghost plant (*Graptopetalum paraguayense*), 19, 21, 25
giant cardon (*Pachycereus pringlei*), 16, 95, 97
giant red aeonium (*Aeonium* 'Cyclops'), 44, 129
giant tree aloe (*Aloe barberae*, aka *Aloidendron barberae*), 62, 64, 66, 149

giant velvet rose aeonium (*Aeonium canariensis*), 19, 42
golden barrel cactus (*Echinocactus grusonii*), 103, 107, 109
golden-flowered century plant (*Agave chrysantha*), 166
golden torch (*Echinopsis spachiana*), 109
goldmoss stonecrop (*Sedum acre*), 35
gophers, 140, 149
Graptopetalum paraguayense (ghost plant), 19, 21, 25
Graptosedum 'Rosa' (Rosa graptosedum), 37
Graptoveria 'David Cumming' (David Cumming graptoveria), 37
G. 'Fred Ives', 50, 117
Greene's dudleya (*Dudleya greenei*), 48
green platters (*Aeonium* 'Pseudotabuliforme'), 44, 55
Grevillea (spider flower), 114
G. *lanigera* 'Prostrate' (prostrate woolly grevillea), 129
Griffin, Kelly, 8, 60
gypsum century plant (*Agave gypsophila*), 127, 164, 165

H

Hartweg's sundrops (*Calylophus hartwegii*), 125
Havard's century plant (*Agave havardiana*), 166
hedgehog cacti (*Echinopsis*), 2
hemp agave. *See* sisal agave
hens and chicks, 7, 48, 50, 52–53, 163
Hesperaloe parvifolia (red yucca), 92, 166
Hesperoyucca, 92
H. *whipplei*. *See Yucca whipplei*
huachuma. See San Pedro cactus
Hummel's Sunset jade plant (*Crassula ovata* 'Hummel's Sunset'), 21
hyssop (*Agastache*), 120

I

ice plants (*Delosperma*), 7
insects, 148–49
irrigation, 142–43, 145–46, 150
island mazanita (*Arctostaphylos insularis* 'Canyon Sparkles'), 127

J

Jaws agave (*Agave gentryi* 'Jaws'), 91, 166
jelly bean stonecrop (*Sedum pachyphyllum*), 21
Joshua tree (*Yucca brevifolia*), 91, 120, 166
Jovibarba, 167
Jurassic Hillside (garden project), 109

K

Kalanchoe beharensis 'Fang' (stalactite plant), 28, 37
K. daigremontiana (mother of thousands), 19
K. fedtschenkoi (lavender scallops), 11
K. marmorata (penwiper plant), 11
K. 'Oak Leaf', 169
K. orgyalis (copper spoons), 28
K. tomentosa (panda plant), 14
Kemble, Brian, 8
King Ferdinand century plant (*Agave nickelsiae*), 166
Kiwi aeonium (*Aeonium* 'Kiwi'), 35, 42, 44
Kluver, April and Ryk, 109
Kniphofia 'Shining Sceptre (orange hot poker), 79, 80

L

lace hedgehog cactus (*Echinocereus reichenbachii*), 167
Latte Rose echeveria (*Echeveria* 'Latte Rose'), 50, 57
lavender scallops (*Kalanchoe fedtschenkoi*), 11
leaf cuttings, 162
lesser Mexican stonecrop (*Sedum confusum*), 167
Leucadendron (conebushes), 62, 116–17

L. 'Jester' (sunshine conebush), 113, 116
L. 'Pom Pom', viii
L. 'Safari Sunset' (Safari Sunset conebush), 107, 116–17
L. salignum 'Summer Red' (Summer Red conebush), 43, 116
Leucospermum (pincushions), 114–15
L. 'Scarlet Ribbon', 112
Leymus condensatus 'Canyon Prince' (Canyon Prince wild rye), 127
lipstick echeveria (*Echeveria agavoides*), 50, 53, 121
live-forevers (*Dudleya*), 43, 44–48
Lobelia laxiflora (Mexican lobelia), 121, 125

M

maiden's quiver tree (*Aloe ramosissima*), 77
Marina strawberry tree (*Arbutus* 'Marina'), 79, 129, 155
mealybugs, 148
Melaleuca nesophila (pink melaleuca), 129
Mexican lobelia (*Lobelia laxiflora*), 121, 125
Mexican snowball (*Echeveria elegans*), 35, 37, 41, 50, 53, 55, 57, 159, 163
Mexican weeping bamboo (*Otatea acuminata aztecorum*), 14
miniature pine tree (*Crassula tetragona*), 19
mirror bush (*Coprosma*), 35, 117
mites, 148, 149
monstrose apple cactus (*Cereus peruvianus* f. *monstrose*), 2, 94
Moonglow aloe (*Aloe* 'Moonglow'), 62, 79, 80, 149
Moonlighting (garden project), 79–80
Moroccan mound (*Euphorbia resinifera*), 79, 80, 91
mother of thousands (*Kalanchoe daigremontiana*), 19
mountain agave (*Agave montana*), 77, 166

mountain aloe (*Aloe marlothii*), 59, 60, 70–71
mountain astelia (*Astelia nervosa*), 127
Mozambique tree aloe (*Aloe tongaensis*, aka *Aloidendron tongaensis*), 64, 65
mulch, 137, 150–51
munchkin dudleya (*Dudleya gnoma*), 48
Myrtillocactus geometrizans (blue candle), 91, 109

N

narrow-leaf century plant (*Agave striata*), 166
Nold, Robert, 8
nurseries, 169–70

O

Ocahui agave (*Agave ocahui*), 84–85, 166
October daphne (*Sedum sieboldii*), 167
octopus agave (*Agave vilmoriniana*), 88–89, 164
octopus aloe (*Aloe vilmoriniana*), 74
offsets, 163–64
old man cactus (*Cephalocereus senilis*), 97
old man of the mountain cactus (*Oreocerus*), 6, 167
Opuntia (prickly pear cacti), 2, 8, 101
O. basilaris (beavertail prickly pear), 102, 167
O. cacanapa 'Ellisiana' (spineless prickly pear), 102, 125, 167
O. microdasys (bunny ears cactus), 101
O. polyacantha 'Dark Knight' (Dark Knight prickly pear), 167
O. santa-rita (Santa Rita prickly pear, aka *O. violacea* var. *santa-rita*), 102, 167
O. violacea var. *santa-rita.* See *Opuntia santa-rita*
orange hot poker (*Kniphofia* 'Shining Sceptre'), 79, 80
Oregon stonecrop (*Sedum oreganum*), 7, 167

Oreocerus (old man of the mountain cactus), 6, 167
organ pipe cactus (*Stenocereus*), 97
Otatea acuminata aztecorum (Mexican weeping bamboo), 14
Our Lord's candle (*Yucca whipplei*, aka *Hesperoyucca whipplei*), 166

P

Pachycereus pringlei (giant cardon), 16, 95, 97
Pacific stonecrop (*Sedum divergens*), 7
palmbob aloe (*Aloe elegans*), 8, 68
panda plant (*Kalanchoe tomentosa*), 14
Parkinsonia florida (blue palo verde), 125
Parodia magnifica (ball cactus), 104
Parry's agave (*Agave parryi*), viii, 107, 109, 114, 166
Pediocactus, 8
Penstemon (beardtongue), 120–21
penwiper plant (*Kalanchoe marmorata*), 11
pests, 148–49
pig's ear (*Cotyledon*), 109
Pilosocereus (blue-skinned cactus), 97
pincushions (*Leucospermum*), 114–15
pink fairy duster (*Calliandra eriophylla*), 117
pink melaleuca (*Melaleuca nesophila*), 129
Pinwheel Hearts (garden project), 55
planting, 139–40
ponytail palm (*Beaucarnea recurvata*), 109
pork and beans stonecrop (*Sedum rubrotinctrum*), 21, 25
Portulacaria afra 'Aurea' (elephant food), 31, 117
P. 'Variegata' (variegated elephant food), 25
predators, 148–49
prickly pear cacti. *See Opuntia*

propagation, 159–65
prostrate woolly grevillea (*Grevillea lanigera* 'Prostrate'), 129
pruners, 153

Q

Quadricolor century plant (*Agave lopahanta* 'Quadricolor'), 79, 80, 166
Queen Victoria agave (*Agave victoriae-reginae*), 87, 133, 166
quiver tree (*Aloe dichotoma*, aka *Aloidendron dichotoma*), 21, 64, 67

R

Ray of Light century plant (*Agave attenuata* 'Ray of Light'), 127, 129
red aloe (*Aloe cameronii*), 77
red bird of paradise (*Caesalpinia pulcherrima*), 118
red frills echeveria (*Echeveria* 'Mauna Loa'), 57
red yucca (*Hesperaloe parvifolia*), 92, 166
Restful Retreat (garden project), 129–30
Rhipsalis cereuscula (thread-leaved mistletoe cactus), 6
rhythm, 4
Rosa graptosedum (*Graptosedum* 'Rosa'), 37
Russian stonecrop (*Sedum kamtschaticum*), 167

S

Safari Sunset conebush (*Leucadendron* 'Safari Sunset'), 107, 116–17
saguaro cactus (*Carnegiea gigantea*), 95
Salvia chamaedryoides (germander sage), 111
San Miguel Island buckwheat (*Erigonum grande* var. *rubescens*), 127
San Pedro cactus (*Echinopsis pachanoi*), 6, 97, 100, 104, 109, 167

Santa Rita prickly pear (*Opuntia santa-rita*, aka *O. violacea* var. *santa-rita*), 102, 167
saucer plant (*Aeonium undulatum*), 41, 53
scale, 62
Schlumbergera (Christmas cactus), 94–95
sea lettuce dudleya (*Dudleya caespitosa*), 47, 48
Secret Passage (garden project), 19
Sedum acre (goldmoss stonecrop), 35
S. adolphi Firestorm, 62
S. 'Angelina', 14
S. confusum (lesser Mexican stonecrop), 167
S. dasyphyllum (Corsican stonecrop), 167
S. divergens (Pacific stonecrop), 7
S. hispanicum (tiny buttons stonecrop), 37
S. kamtschaticum (Russian stonecrop), 167
S. nussbaumerianum 'Coppertone' (Coppertone stonecrop), 21, 31, 35, 73, 74, 161
S. oreganum (Oregon stonecrop), 7, 167
S. pachyphyllum (jelly bean stonecrop), 21
S. reflexum 'Blue Spruce' (Blue Spruce stonecrop), 21, 74
S. rubrotinctrum (pork and beans stonecrop), 21, 25
S. sieboldii (October daphne), 167
S. spathulifolium (broadleaf stonecrop), 7, 167
S. stenopetalum (wormleaf stonecrop), 7
Sempervivum, 7, 163, 167
Senecio mandraliscae (blue chalk sticks), 19, 25
S. radicans (fish hooks), 31, 37
S. rowleyanus (string of pearls), 35, 37
Senna artemisioides (feathery cassia), 118
S. phyllodinea (silver leaf cassia), 118

shin daggers (*Agave lechuguilla*), 166
shovels, 155–56
Sierra Mixteca agave (*Agave oteroi* 'Felipe Otero'), 79, 80
silver leaf cassia (*Senna phyllodinea*), 118
silver torch cactus (*Cleistocactus strausii*), 97, 167
sisal agave (*Agave sisalana*), 163
Sleek Lines and Spines (garden project), 107
Slim bottlebrush (*Callistemon viminalis* 'Slim'), 129
small gardens
designing, 11–14, 16
projects, 19, 21–22
smooth agave (*Agave desmetiana*), 89, 117, 164
soaptree yucca (*Yucca elata*), 91
soapweed (*Yucca glauca*), 91, 166
soil, 134–37
spades, 155–56
Spanish dagger (*Yucca aloifolia*), 166
spider aloe (*Aloe bracteosa*), 74
spider flower (*Grevillea*), 114
spineless prickly pear (*Opuntia cacanapa* 'Ellisiana'), 102, 125, 167
squid agave (*Agave bracteosa*), 85, 166
stalactite plant (*Kalanchoe beharensis* 'Fang'), 28, 37
Starr, Greg, 8
stem cuttings, 160–61
Stenocereus (organ pipe cactus), 97
stone, 137
stonecrops, 41. *See also individual species*
string of pearls (*Senecio rowleyanus*), 35, 37
succulents
advantages of, viii, 1
cacti vs., 2
climate and, 6–8, 27, 146, 166–67
companion plants for, 122–23
etymology of, 2

planting, 139–40
propagating, 159–65
watering, vii–viii, 1, 6, 83, 142–43, 145–46, 150
See also individual plants
Summer Red conebush (*Leucadendron salignum* 'Summer Red'), 43, 116
sunset aloe (*Aloe dorotheae*), 72–73, 75, 149
sunshine conebush (*Leucadendron* 'Jester'), 113, 116

T
Texas barrel cactus (*Ferocactus hamatacanthus*), 167
Texas yucca. *See* red yucca
texture, 14
Thamm, Leo, 60, 79
thread agave (*Agave filifera*), 91
thread-leaved mistletoe cactus (*Rhipsalis cereuscula*), 6
tilt-head aloe (*Aloe speciosa*), 68, 71–72
tiny buttons stonecrop (*Sedum hispanicum*), 37
tools
caring for, 156
for digging, 155–56
for pruning, 153
quality of, 152
suppliers of, 171
for weeding, 151–52
toothless torch aloe (*Aloe arborescens* 'Spineless'), 21
Trager, John, 8
twin-flowered agave (*Agave geminiflora*), 4, 86

U
Utah agave (*Agave utahensis*), 166

V
Van Balen's aloe (*Aloe vanbalenii*), 74–75
variegated elephant food (*Portulacaria* 'Variegata'), 25
viviparous foxtail cactus (*Escobaria vivipara* var. *rosea*), 167

W
Walska, Ganna, 72
Washingtonia filifera (California fan palm), 103
watering, 142–43, 145–46, 150
weak-leaf yucca (*Yucca flaccida*), 91, 93
weeds, 150–52
Welcome Home (garden project), 127
whale's tongue agave (*Agave ovatifolia*), 14, 91, 166
white cloud echeveria (*Echeveria cante*), 57
woolly bush (*Adenanthos sericeus*), 35
wormleaf stonecrop (*Sedum stenopetalum*), 7

Y
yellow bird of paradise (*Caesalpinia gilliesii*), 118
Yucca
characteristics of, 91
cold-hardy, 166
Y. aloifolia (Spanish dagger), 166
Y. baccata (banana yucca), 91, 166
Y. brevifolia (Joshua tree), 91, 120, 166
Y. Bright Star (Bright Star yucca), 14, 24, 91, 115, 166
Y. desmetiana 'Blue Boy' (Blue Boy yucca), 91, 115, 166
Y. elata (soaptree yucca), 91
Y. filamentosa 'Colorguard' (Color Guard yucca), 93, 166
Y. flaccida (weak-leaf yucca), 91, 93
Y. glauca (soapweed), 91, 166
Y. rostrata (beaked yucca), 93, 103, 166
Y. whipplei (Our Lord's candle, aka *Hesperoyucca whipplei*), 166

Z
Zimbabwe aloe (*Aloe excelsa*), vii, 60, 77

Published in the United States by Ten Speed Press, an imprint of
Random House, a division of Penguin Random House LLC, New York.
www.tenspeed.com

Ten Speed Press and the Ten Speed Press colophon are registered trademarks
of Penguin Random House LLC.

Library of Congress Cataloging-in-Publication Data
    Names: Frank, Gabriel, 1978- author.
    Title: Striking succulent gardens : plants and plans for designing your
        low-maintenance landscape / Gabriel Frank.
    Description: First edition. | Emeryville, California : Ten Speed Press, 2020. |
        Includes index.
    Identifiers: LCCN 2020011706 (print) | LCCN 2020011707 (ebook) |
        ISBN 9780399580987 (trade paperback) | ISBN 9780399580994 (ebook)
    Subjects: LCSH: Gardening. | Landscape gardening. | Mediterranean climate. |
        Succulent plants.
    Classification: LCC SB454.3.M43 F73 2020 (print) | LCC SB454.3.M43
        (ebook) | DDC 635—dc23
    LC record available at https://lccn.loc.gov/2020011706
    LC ebook record available at https://lccn.loc.gov/2020011707

Trade Paperback ISBN: 978-0-399-58098-7
eBook ISBN: 978-0-399-58099-4

Printed in China

Photography Credits
    Gabriel Frank: pages 43, 46 (left), 88, 90 (middle row center and right; bottom
    row center), 97, 102 (center and right), 110, 121 (right), 161 (bottom right)
    John Manning: page 67
    Dominic Gentilcore, PhD/Shutterstock: page 102 (left)
    Meunierd/Shutterstock: page 117
    Iva Villi/Shutterstock: page 118 (top)
    Juntee/Shutterstock: page 121 (left)

Design by Chloe Rawlins

10 9 8 7 6 5 4 3 2 1

First Edition